This book has the most solid teach.
Not only is this message helpful, but it's also refreshingly honest
and carefully researched. This is wisdom I've personally seen Pastor
Derwin live out both through these pages and in everyday life.

Lysa TerKeurst, #1 *New York Times* bestselling
author of *Uninvited* and *It's Not Supposed to Be This Way*,
and president of Proverbs 31 Ministries

From the great sermon in history comes the greatest words on happiness. Jesus' famous Beatitudes have blessed millions upon millions
of people who have searched for true and lasting joy. My friend
Derwin Gray masterfully unpacks the words of Christ with the skill
of a scholar and the heart of a pastor. The result is a book that will
bless a generation that is hungry for the happiness of heaven.

Max Lucado, preaching minister of Oak Hills Church, author
of *How Happiness Happens: Finding Lasting Joy in a World of
Comparison, Disappointment, and Unmet Expectations*

I have watched Derwin Gray hold a room filled with thousands of
college students spellbound as he unpacked the simple, profound,
life-altering implications of the grace of Jesus in our lives. Then I
watched him personally minister one-by-one to a line of hundreds
of students who wanted to walk with Jesus. Thank you for putting
your insights into a book, brother. May God bless us all as we seek
him together!

Ben Stuart, pastor of Passion City Church D.C.
and author of *Single, Dating, Engaged, Married*

Pastor Derwin has done it again! Not many people can so brilliantly weave high-level theology in such easy to understand and practical ways. Pastor Derwin and this book are a gift and surely will leave you feeling encouraged and equipped!

Jefferson Bethke, *New York Times* bestselling author of *Jesus > Religion*

I found such depth in the principles of *The Good Life*—an incredible perspective shift for happiness cravers, everywhere. Derwin has nailed it with this book. The wise teaching and candid storytelling bring the same power as hearing him preach!

Lisa Whittle, author of *Jesus Over Everything*, Bible teacher, and cofounder of Called Creatives

Pastor Derwin has played a powerful role in teaching me the true essence of Christ's love. Many know that I was raised in the "church" and have carried God with me every step of the way. But the Scripture based teachings and the compassionate delivery that I receive from Pastor Derwin have caused me to revisit the understandings that I once had and have allowed me to open up so much more to God's truth and unfailing love for me as a true believer. I highly recommend my pastor's book, *The Good Life*. Read and let God transform your life.

Fantasia, American Idol Winner, Grammy Award winner

Derwin Gray has written a gem, a book that reminds me of my own quest and conquest of that elusive thing called happiness. Like me, Derwin found happiness in Jesus Christ. Yet sadly, many

Christians lack happiness too. So what gives? You'll find the answer in the pages of this book. Taking words straight from the author of happiness, Jesus Himself, Derwin lays out the blueprint for a happy and fulfilling life. Reading *The Good Life* will make you think; it'll make you smile, and most of all, it'll make you happy—forever.

Chris Broussard, FOX Sports Broadcaster,
founder and president of The K.I.N.G. Movement

In *The Good Life*, Derwin Gray reflects on the Beatitudes and shows how a life of faith and fruitfulness flows from the surprising grace of the gospel. Here is a book that will encourage you, challenge you, and equip you to be a demonstration of the grace and power of God!

Trevin Wax, senior vice president of
Theology and Communications at LifeWay Christian Resources,
author of *This Is Our Time* and *Rethink Your Self*

The Good Life, by my friend Derwin Gray, is about happiness sought, happiness found, and happiness deepened. It is the story of a man who has found the love of God, the love of others, and the love of self personally, and who through that personal encounter with the God of the good life has found the Beatitudes of Jesus as they are meant to be seen: as people who truly know God and through knowing God know themselves and how to love others. *The Good Life* is a timely warning to America about its obsession with what is not good and an instruction for the church to chase after the good God who alone knows what the good life is. We see that good life in Jesus and Derwin takes us to him.

Rev. Canon Dr. Scot McKnight,
professor of New Testament, Northern Seminary

Derwin Gray's latest book, *The Good Life: What Jesus Teaches about Finding True Happiness* brilliantly combines true to life stories and truth of Scripture to help us discover what we all long for—true happiness. Derwin masterfully takes the ancient words of Jesus in the Beatitudes and brings them into our contemporary world to show us how the good life is possible. If you don't want to settle for mediocrity or so-so living, this is the book for you!

Dave Ferguson, lead pastor of Community
Christian Church and author of *Hero Maker:
Five Essential Practices for Leaders to Multiply Leaders*

I searched for happiness most of my life but was never happy until I found Jesus at the age of thirty-six. That's why I love this book and believe everyone should read it. Dr. Gray explains that Jesus not only provides us with the blueprint for happiness but he is the blueprint. This book is a prescription for overcoming anxiety and fear. We can learn from his teachings, follow his example and most of all find true happiness through a relationship with him. Thankfully Dr. Gray guides us on this journey to the good life. It's a journey I encourage you to take and Dr. Gray is an amazing guide.

Jon Gordon, bestselling author of *The Carpenter and The Seed*

If Derwin Gray is speaking or writing, I always pay attention. Derwin is my trusted friend and his words are uniquely prophetic, powerful, and penetrating. I love this book and it will help all of us discover the truth about happiness.

Pastor Brady Boyd, New Life Church, Colorado Springs and
author of *Addicted to Busy and Remarkable*

There are three things I appreciate about this book: One, it's helpful, but not self-help. Its practical AND biblical, a very difficult thing to find these days. I appreciate the real life teaching that Dr. Gray shares with us. Two, is the book's Christology. The pages are dripping with Jesus and you can't help to be drenched in his grace through the reading. Finally, authorship matters. The author is a Christian. The public persona and his private values match. His character, passion for the lost and a never-tiring effort to reflect here on earth the values God designed in heaven, makes this book a must read because it comes from a place of experience not theory. You will be blessed as you read it.

Roger Hernandez, ministerial and
evangelism director, Southern Union Conference

So many of us are pursuing happiness in an age where it feels more and more elusive. Derwin's story and writing is filled with heart, passion and real-life experience that points you to the ultimate source. If your soul is hungry, you've come to the right place.

Carey Nieuwhof, founding pastor of
Connexus Church and author of *Didn't See It Coming*

In our current times, there is so much hunger and thirst for this thing we call "happiness" and there is no shortage of answers coming from the world. But what does God have to say about happiness? In blending personal stories with sound theological teaching, Derwin does a masterful job exploring what it actually looks like to live the good life and find true, lasting happiness.

Albert Tate, founder and lead pastor of Fellowship Church

As apprentices of Jesus, you and I need guides who have received and are willing to share divine wisdom with us. Dr. Gray provides guidance to us and *The Good Life* contains wisdom for us. I hope you'll join me in marinating on what you read and sharing the happiness of God with others.

Pastor Matt Adair, Christ Community Church, Athens, Georgia

This book contains a helpful mix of pastoral insight that comes from years of ministry, vivid story telling, and sound biblical interpretation. Derwin uses the Beatitudes to challenge our infatuation with the false pursuit of happiness rooted in the American Dream. Instead he calls us to follow the man from Nazareth the fount of all our joy. Church leaders and lay people will benefit from a close reading and reflection on what he has to say.

Esau McCaulley, PhD, assistant professor
of New Testament, Wheaton College

DR. DERWIN L. GRAY

the good life

WHAT JESUS TEACHES ABOUT FINDING TRUE HAPPINESS

foreword by Beth Moore

B&H
PUBLISHING
NASHVILLE, TENNESSEE

978-1-5359-9571-9

Published by B&H Publishing Group
Nashville, Tennessee

Dewey Decimal: 248.84
Subject Heading: HAPPINESS / CHRISTIAN LIFE /
BEATITUDES

Cover design by A. Micah Smith.
Author photo © Transformation Church.

Published in association with The Bindery Agency,
www.TheBinderyAgency.com.

1 2 3 4 5 6 7 • 24 23 22 21 20

I dedicate this book to Presley Ann Gray, my first-born, my daughter, my warrior-princess. I wasn't going to write this book. I was feeling insecure about my ability to write. However, feelings of insecurity transformed to feelings of confidence and a sense of divine calling after my daughter spoke some life-giving words to me.

On a family trip to Oslo, Norway, last spring I shared with my wife and kids the reasons why I thought I shouldn't write this book. Thankfully, my daughter, a psychology major, spoke truth to my heart. She basically told me, "Dad, if God is calling you to write this book, you are ultimately writing it as an act of worship and expression of love to him. Don't let feelings of insecurity and things you can't control keep you from doing what you know you are called to do." I knew she was right, so I started to write.

Presley, I dedicate *The Good Life: What Jesus Teaches about Finding True Happiness* to you. Thank you for making me a better follower of Jesus and a better dad. I love you to Jupiter and back 480,000,000 times.

Love,
Papi

Acknowledgments

For something significant to be accomplished, it takes the passion and effort of many people. *The Good Life: What Jesus Teaches about Finding True Happiness* is the result of passionate people who have inspired, encouraged, and partnered with me. I'm indebted to my wife and best friend, Vicki. She is my hero. My children, Presley and Jeremiah, are a continual source of encouragement and inspiration, and they make me a better father. I appreciate the editorial Jedi skills of Chris McGinn as well as the assistance of Alex Hoover and Kristel Acevedo. I'm thankful for Taylor Combs and all the B&H Publishing team. I appreciate my agent, Alexander Fields, for believing in me and in this book. Also, I'm thankful for the Transformation Church family. It was your response in 2015 to a sermon series on this topic that inspired the writing of this book.

Last, but definitely not least, I thank God the Father for his faithful love, the Lord Jesus for his lavish grace, and God the Holy Spirit for his wisdom and power. To God alone be the glory.

Dr. Derwin L. Gray
December 17, 2019
Transformation Church, Indian Land, South Carolina

Contents

Foreword

I love Derwin Gray. He is a dear friend and cherished brother in Christ, but those things, as wonderful as they are, would not have wooed me out of foreword-writing retirement. I accepted this privilege and carved out the space for three reasons. First, this guy is one of the most effective Christian leaders I have ever encountered, and I want people to know about him and flourish under his influence. Second, he shares Christ's passion for the multi-ethnic church and has the gifted wherewithal to help willing people move that direction. Third, *The Good Life* is a great book and demonstrates the author's glorious preoccupation with Christ and his gospel, a preoccupation God wills for every person of faith.

I met Derwin for the first time some years ago when our mutual friend, Ed Stetzer, invited us along with several others to be interviewed by him for a television program. Before taping, we got to enjoy a warm, relaxed meal together. A connection happened at that dinner table as it often does between strangers who are related by the blood of Jesus. True kin meet one another for the very first time but, a few hours later, feel that they have known one another all their lives. What impressed me most about Derwin was that he sought to be a student and a servant to every person at that table. He did not draw attention to himself and, goodness knows, it would have been effortless. He is larger than life in every way, magnetic and winsome with a smile as wide as the Lone Star State where he was raised. He drew attention to others. He ministered to us. I learned that night we had a connection through his wife, Vicki, a stellar disciple and servant of Christ in her own right, who'd taken many of my Bible studies. I loved her immediately, sight unseen, and would only love her more when I finally met her face to face.

I watched Derwin from the greenroom at the studio during his time to be interviewed that evening and grew increasingly fascinated. He was bereft of pretense and so alive with passion for the gospel of Jesus Christ that he struggled to stay seated. I read his first book within the next couple of days then followed him on social media and into his ongoing world. The rest is Gray-Moore history. We three—Derwin, Vicki, and me—bonded for life.

I love the local church and have no few favorites, but Transformation Church, the fellowship of believers Derwin pastors, is in my top three picks of all times. It houses that rare but God-intended fusion of Word and Spirit. Of grace and truth. Of intellect and emotion. Of delight and devotion. It's a place where you are continually taught and reminded of the immeasurable, unconditional love of God yet also called to repentance of sins that cheat you of abundant life and fruitfulness. That's Transformation Church because that's Derwin Gray.

He's brilliant and funny and self-deprecating and insightful. And, while he's a gentleman and a scholar, he also has some impressive moves and sometimes breaks them down right in the middle of a sermon. But best of all, as you open this book, Derwin knows what he's talking about. If somebody's going to teach me about finding true happiness, let it be a person I'm convinced has discovered a healthy measure of it.

Prepare to learn and be challenged. Get ready to grow and be stretched and go ahead and thank God in advance that, if you're willing, you are about to enter a happier, more fulfilling life. Forget fairy tales. Forget the carnal pleasures that make big promises but can't even keep them through the weekend. Embrace the way of Jesus Christ, the savior of the world. Grab onto the gospel and really live.

You're in good hands here.

Beth Moore

CHAPTER 1

Chasing Shadows

As a little boy growing up on the west side of San Antonio, Texas, I loved chasing my shadow. Back in the late 1970s, children didn't have smartphones or tablets to entertain us, so we played outside, making up games as daylight slipped into night. Chasing my shadow always started fun, but the enjoyment soon faded into frustration when I realized I could never catch it, no matter how fast I ran.

Trying to find lasting happiness is like chasing your shadow; what starts as childish fun erodes into adult frustration, failure, and disappointment.

At some point in our lives, we realize no matter how hard and how long we work, we will never catch lasting happiness. Just when you think the new boyfriend will give you lasting happiness, he dumps you. Just when you think the new job is going to give you what you want, frustrations with your boss leave you longing for a better one. You go on an epic vacation and see things you've never seen, but by the time you get on the plane, your happy feelings are slipping through your hands like grains of sand.

But this is the home of the American Dream. We are entitled to happiness, right? We've been told that if we work hard enough, do the right things, get the right education, get the right career, marry the right spouse, have a few kids, and live in a nice house, we will be happy.

The pursuit of happiness is even written into the DNA of America. Way back in 1776, the Founding Fathers wrote in the Declaration of Independence: "We hold these truths to be self-evident, that all men are created equal, that they are endowed by their Creator with certain unalienable Rights, that among these are Life, Liberty and *the pursuit of Happiness.*" There it is—*the pursuit of happiness.* The good life is ours for the taking if only we can catch it and keep it. But catching it is like chasing shadows. No matter how fast we run, it always seems to be just beyond our reach. After a while, we stop reaching and just settle.

My American Dream

If there were a picture of the American Dream on Wikipedia, it would be of my big ol' head. I'm the son of two African-American teenagers from the hood. My parents brought me into the world at a time when heroin and crack flooded poor communities. I experienced things no child should ever have to experience or even know about. But I had a dream.

During my freshman year of high school, I was inspired by a senior football player. He earned a football scholarship to a major university, and if that wasn't enough, the prettiest girl in the school was his girlfriend. He was living the good life—he was happy. And I wanted to be happy too.

After practice, under the scorching South Texas sun, I overheard our head football coach say that the senior player that I admired had transformed his body over the summer with weight and plyometric training. I thought to myself, *He's from the hood just like me. If he can train hard and transform his body, get a scholarship, and get the prettiest girl in school, so can I.* As silly as that sounds, I'll never forget that day, because that was the day I decided I would do whatever it took to be good enough at football to earn a scholarship. I wanted the good life.

During my sophomore year, I transferred to Converse Judson High School. Judson was a football dynasty. My head coach, D. W. Rutledge, and my defensive back coach, Mike Sullivan, taught me more than football. These men taught my teammates and me life skills like the value of hard work, discipline, resilience, dedication, sacrifice, and teamwork. As I bought into Judson's culture, I went from a scrawny, weak, slow kid to a strong, muscular, fast, elite athlete garnering the attention of college football scouts. Eventually, the dream came to fruition. I accepted a football scholarship to Brigham Young University (BYU). However, before I could gain admission into BYU, I had to academically qualify by scoring a 16 on the ACT.

Coach Sullivan made sure I was prepared for the ACT. Several times a week, he had me work on a computer program that prepared students to take the test. I took the ACT three times before I finally scored the magic number of 16. I was the first person in my family to go to college; my family was so proud of me. I was on my way to lasting happiness

Provo, Utah, where BYU is located, is breathtakingly beautiful. The campus is situated below the majestic Wasatch Mountains. As a South Texas kid, the beauty of Provo captured me. But then I saw something more beautiful than the mountains—a girl with a long ponytail lifting weights in the BYU athletic weight room. We spoke briefly, but she was focused. No time to flirt.

A few weeks went by, and I saw her playing pickup basketball with other BYU athletes. After the game, I found out she was a javelin thrower on the track team. I found this beautiful and mesmerizing all at once. She could hug me with her strong arms, and she could kill me with her javelin—what a woman! We chatted for about an hour after the game, but she told me she had a boyfriend, so I backed off.

Another few weeks went by and I saw her again. I jokingly said, "Do you still have that boyfriend?" To my surprise, she told me she didn't. We exchanged phone numbers and, well, the rest is history. Vicki and I have been together ever since. On May 23, 2020, we celebrated twenty-eight years of marriage.

My BYU experience was great. I'm recognized as one of the greatest players ever to have played at BYU, and I married Superwoman. My dream came true, and I was living the good life.

I was happy . . . at least for a little while.

Still Haven't Found What I'm Looking For

Dreams do come true. On April 25, 1993, the Indianapolis Colts drafted me as the 92nd selection in the NFL Draft. It was surreal. I did it. I was living the American Dream. *The good life and happiness will be mine,* I thought. But just like chasing shadows as a little boy, I really wouldn't be able to truly catch lasting happiness.

My first year in the NFL was miserable. I didn't have many friends on the team. I was barely playing. Some of my teammates didn't like me because my wife was white. My wife and I were both lonely. We wanted to go back to BYU where I was a beloved star.

My second year was better, and by my third year, I was the Special Teams Captain. I was now a valuable member of the team, and people in the city knew me for my community service. But my marriage wasn't good, and the happiness that I wanted continued to elude me. I was famous, I had the girl, I had the money, yet it made my life worse because I was supposed to be happy, and I wasn't. If this was the good life, it was an epic letdown.

> **I WAS FAMOUS, I HAD THE GIRL, I HAD THE MONEY, YET IT MADE MY LIFE WORSE BECAUSE I WAS SUPPOSED TO BE HAPPY, AND I WASN'T.**

Don't get me wrong; there were happy moments; but like you, I was looking for a happiness that was more than just feeling good from time to time. Like you, I wanted a happiness deeper, better, and more real than that. Like the U2 song, I still hadn't found what I was looking for.

My Story, Your Story, Our Story

My story of seeking happiness in jobs, relationships, fame, and money is not much different than most people in our culture. In 2008, *four thousand* books were written on the topic of happiness, up from just fifty in 2000.[1] "According to some measures, as a nation we've grown sadder and more anxious during the same years that the happiness movement has flourished,"[2] wrote Carlin Flora of *Psychology Today*. To highlight the unhappiness in our culture, Yale University now offers a class on the subject that has become the most popular class in the prestigious school's history.[3] Almost 25 percent of Yale's undergrads take the course, "Psyc 157, Psychology and the Good Life."[4] Dr. Laurie Santos, who teaches it, writes, "Students want to change, to be happier themselves, and to change the culture here on campus."[5] A Yale undergrad who took the course said, "In reality, a lot of us are anxious, stressed, unhappy, numb."[6] Even Bristol University in England is offering a twelve-week course in "How to Achieve Happiness."[7] The course explores topics from "psychology, neuroscience, and will explore ways to achieve true happiness, how to live fulfilling lives."[8]

As a pastor, I see a lot of unhappy people. With more than fifteen years of counseling experience, I have learned that both those who follow Jesus and those who do not are longing and desperately searching for happiness. In their search, many are learning all the places where it can't be found: a career, a marriage, in sexual escapades, in having children, in partying, or anything else. C. S. Lewis, a former atheist who became one of the most beloved Christians of the twentieth century, was on to something when he wrote:

> If I find in myself a desire which no experience in
> this world can satisfy, the most probable explana-
> tion is that I was made for another world. If none
> of my earthly pleasures satisfy it, that does not
> prove that the universe is a fraud. Probably earthly
> pleasures were never meant to satisfy it, but only
> to arouse it, to suggest the real thing.[9]

What if the happiness we are hustling after can never be caught?

What if the happiness we are running ourselves into physical, mental, and emotional exhaustion for is inferior to the happiness we've been made to experience?

What if created things were never meant to make us happy in the way we desire to experience happiness?

I believe the ancient Jewish people knew the secret to happiness. Marinate on the words to these two songs they would sing to God and to each other as a reminder of where happiness is found:

WHAT IF THE HAPPINESS WE ARE HUSTLING AFTER CAN NEVER BE CAUGHT?

> Happy are the people who know the joyful shout; LORD, they walk in the light from your face. They rejoice in your name all day long, and they are exalted by your righteousness. (Ps. 89:15–16)

> You reveal the path of life to me; in your presence is abundant joy; at your right hand are eternal pleasures. (Ps. 16:11)

What if happiness is found by gazing into the face of God in Jesus Christ, and walking in his path of light, life, and righteousness?

The Happiest Man That Ever Lived

Jesus of Nazareth was the happiest person who ever lived. He is the ultimate portrait of the good life. He is the prototype of what humanity was meant to be. The first Adam cursed humanity by his disobedience in the garden of Eden; Jesus, the last Adam, reversed the curse through his obedience. The first Adam brought us death; the last Adam brought us back to life.

No matter the situation, whether feeding five thousand men or driving corrupt people out of the temple or hanging in agony on a Roman cross, Jesus had transcendent happiness that gave him confidence and purpose. His happiness rooted him in something deeper, better, and more beautiful than his circumstances. *Jesus' circumstances were not the cause of his happiness, nor did they add or subtract from his happiness; they were the window through which he expressed his happiness.* His happiness was a different kind of joy that seemed to come from a realm beyond ours. Here's how the author of Hebrews described it:

> For the joy that lay before him, he endured the
> cross, despising the shame, and sat down at the
> right hand of the throne of God. (Heb. 12:2)

The word translated *joy* is the Greek word *chará,* and it means a state of gladness or happiness. How can a person be happy after being stripped naked in public, tied over a wooden beam, and flogged with a flagrum? The flagrum was comprised of leather straps with sharp pieces of bone and metal embedded at the end of the leather straps. It would grip into the victim's body and rip the flesh. How could Jesus be in a state of gladness as a hurricane of torture engulfed him at every level of his being?

By the time Jesus was on earth, the Romans had perfected the art of death by crucifixion. The cross is one of the most heinous ways ever invented for a man to die. It was brutal, painful, and slow. It was a symbol of domination and devastation. Dying by the cross was so cruel that neither a Roman citizen nor a woman could be crucified. Yet, Jesus was able to have joy during his public execution. How? Jesus knew the secret to happiness. Jesus knew that his happiness had to be entrenched in something that was beyond this world but that gave him the grace to live here.

Jesus is able to have this happiness because he is the true version of humanity. Salvation is the restoration of our humanity, and along with our humanness being reestablished in Christ, we gain the capacity to experience real happiness, the God-kind-of-happiness that is reserved for citizens of his kingdom.

The happiness of Jesus is available to us.

The Beatitudes

For thirty-three years, Jesus was happiness personified. He came to earth on a mission of reconciliation, with a royal invitation in his bloody, nail-pierced hands. He was inviting us to experience his kind of happiness, as citizens in his kingdom. Here's the invitation card:

> "Blessed are the poor in spirit,
> for the kingdom of heaven is theirs.
> Blessed are those who mourn,
> for they will be comforted.
> Blessed are the humble,
> for they will inherit the earth.
> Blessed are those who hunger and thirst for
> righteousness,
> for they will be filled.
> Blessed are the merciful,

for they will be shown mercy.
Blessed are the pure in heart,
for they will see God.
Blessed are the peacemakers,
for they will be called sons of God.
Blessed are those who are persecuted because of
    righteousness,
for the kingdom of heaven is theirs.

You are blessed when they insult you and persecute you and falsely say every kind of evil against
you because of me. Be glad and rejoice, because
your reward is great in heaven. For that is how
they persecuted the prophets who were before
you." (Matt. 5:3–12)

This passage is known as "The Beatitudes." Through his words,
Jesus takes a blank canvas and begins to paint a portrait that is so
moving that, by gazing at it, we are somehow transported into a different world—a better, more beautiful, life-giving world. I suspect
one of the reasons that movie sagas series like The Lord of the Rings,
Harry Potter, and Star Wars have worldwide success is because these
movies take us to a different realm in which we reimagine our
existence. The Beatitudes are a description of how God's kingdom
enters man's realm and transforms it. The Beatitudes are a picture
of what God's people, under his rule and reign of grace, live like on
earth. They are the ethos of heaven invading earth. It's like God's
people bring the currency of heaven and spend it on earth, enriching
everyone's life.

The apostle Paul describes the riches of God's kingdom as "righteousness, peace, and joy in the Holy Spirit" (Rom. 14:17). Joy or happiness is the fragrance of God's kingdom. Think about these words:

> For to God, we are the fragrance of Christ among those who are being saved and among those who are perishing. To some we are an aroma of death leading to death, but to others, an aroma of life leading to life. (2 Cor. 2:15–16)

Jesus is the embodiment of the Beatitudes.[10] He was humble and poor. His short life has had lasting endurance because he spent it pursuing God's justice and righteousness. Jesus, the Prince of Peace, brought the peace of God everywhere he went. His shed blood on the cross transformed enemies into friends, failures into successes, and cowards into conquering apostles. What a gracious God we serve.

Jesus not only shows us the way to happiness by his life's example; he also teaches and empowers us to do the same. In an act of mind-blowing grace, he shares his good and eternal life with us, so we can grow into the people of God who embody the Beatitudes. Jesus is a good king, he would never ask us to do something that he does not first provide the grace to accomplish. Where God guides, God provides.

JESUS NOT ONLY SHOWS US THE WAY TO HAPPINESS BY HIS LIFE'S EXAMPLE, HE ALSO TEACHES AND EMPOWERS US TO DO THE SAME.

"I am the vine; you are the branches. The one who *remains in me and I in him* produces much fruit, because you can do nothing without me." (John 15:5, emphasis mine)

I have been crucified with Christ, and I no longer live, *but Christ lives in me.* The life I now live in the body, I live by faith in the Son of God, who loved me and gave himself for me. (Gal. 2:20, emphasis mine)

I labor for this, striving with *his strength* that works powerfully in me. (Col. 1:29, emphasis mine)

For it is *God who is working in you* both to will and to work according to his good purpose. (Phil. 2:13, emphasis mine)

Now to him who is able to do above and beyond all that we ask or think according to *the power that works in us*—to him be glory in the church and in Christ Jesus to all generations, forever and ever. Amen. (Eph. 3:20–21, emphasis mine)

Love in Action

The Beatitudes are what love looks like in action.

One day an expert in the Jewish law (or Torah, which is the first five books of the Old Testament) attempted to trick Jesus and expose him as a false prophet. This is funny considering that

Jesus is the author of the Torah and lived it perfectly. He was being questioned with the intent of trapping him. Imagine trying to trick Einstein in math, or trying to teach Michael Jackson to dance or Denzel Washington to act! This is pure silliness. Nevertheless, Jesus plays along the way we play along with children when we know that they have no clue what they are talking about.

The Torah expert asks Jesus what commandments are the most important. Jesus responds by saying:

> "Love the Lord your God with all your heart, with all your soul, and with all your mind. This is the greatest and most important command. The second is like it: Love your neighbor as yourself. All the Law and the Prophets depend on these two commands." (Matt. 22:37–40)

The Torah expert told Jesus that he answered correctly (Mark 12:32–33). I wonder if Jesus was laughing in his mind thinking, *Of course I answered correctly. I wrote it!*

When Jesus answered the question, he was forming what my doctoral advisor and New Testament scholar Scot McKnight calls the Jesus Creed.[11] Jesus combined Deuteronomy 6:4–9 and Leviticus 19:9–18 into this one command. Jesus communicates that the entire Torah is summed up in these simple commands: love God, love self, and love neighbor. A fully *transformed* human is one who can love God, self, and neighbor through God's presence and power, and by participating in the eternal-kind-of-life of Jesus.

Often people wonder what it looks like to "love my neighbor." Jesus' audience would have known from the writings in the Old Testament such as Leviticus 19:

"When you reap the harvest of your land, you are not to reap to the very edge of your field or gather the gleanings of your harvest. Do not strip your vineyard bare or gather its fallen grapes. Leave them for the poor and the resident alien; I am the LORD your God.

"Do not steal. Do not act deceptively or lie to one another. Do not swear falsely by my name, profaning the name of your God; I am the LORD.

"Do not oppress your neighbor or rob him. The wages due a hired worker must not remain with you until morning. Do not curse the deaf or put a stumbling block in front of the blind, but you are to fear your God; I am the LORD.

"Do not act unjustly when deciding a case. Do not be partial to the poor or give preference to the rich; judge your neighbor fairly. Do not go about spreading slander among your people; do not jeopardize your neighbor's life; I am the LORD.

"Do not harbor hatred against your brother. Rebuke your neighbor directly, and you will not incur guilt because of him. Do not take revenge or bear a grudge against members of your community, but love your neighbor as yourself; I am the LORD." (vv. 9–18)

Here's my paraphrase:

> In response to God's generous love, generously provide for the poor.

In response to God's grace, don't take what's not yours or lie to people for dishonest gain.

In response to God's kindness, treat people kindly; if not, you are dishonoring God's name.

In response to God's mercy, don't oppress people by cheating them financially.

In response to God's goodness, protect those with special needs and those who are marginalized.

In response to God's justice, don't suck up to the rich while being unfair and unjust to the poor.

In response to God's truth, don't slander or gossip about people. Words cut deep like a sharp blade.

In response to God's forgiveness, forgive those who have hurt you.

In response to the cross, do not carry a grudge; it's far too heavy. Give it to me. You'll be happier.

I am the Lord, your God. Love people the way I have loved you; this is why I made you. Don't worry—if you rest in me, my strength will be yours. I'll do this in you and through you. I am

the Lord, your God. I am good. I will give you
my goodness. This is the good life. This is true
happiness.

To love our neighbors is to love God. To love God requires that
we love our neighbors.

Good grief. I'm convicted.

Upward, Inward, Outward

Loving God, self, and our neighbor looks like the Beatitudes.
What Scot McKnight calls the Jesus Creed, theologian Ken Boa
calls "Upward, Inward, Outward."[12]

Upward

Loving God completely is a growth process that involves the
personal elements of communication and response. By listening to
the Holy Spirit in the words of Scripture and speaking to the Lord
in our thoughts and prayers, we move in the direction of knowing
him better. The better we know him, the more we will love him,
and the more we love him, the greater will be our willingness to
respond to him in trust and obedience.

Inward

To love ourselves correctly is to see ourselves as God sees us and
to allow the Word, not the world, to define who and whose we really
are. The clearer we capture the vision of our new identity in Jesus
Christ, the more we will realize that our deepest needs for security,

significance, and satisfaction are met in him and not in people, possessions, or positions.

Outward

A biblical view of our identity and resources in Christ moves us in the direction of loving others compassionately. Grasping our true and unlimited resources in Christ frees us from bondage to the opinions of others and gives us the liberty to love and serve others regardless of their response.

To say that the concept of "Upward, Inward, Outward" has been epic in my life is not strong enough. Once the Spirit of God grasped my heart with this truth, I began to see how just as God is triune (the Father, the Son, and the Holy Spirit), love itself is triune (Upward, Inward, Outward). As I spent time with Jesus, he became more beautiful and more real to me every day. The more I got to know him through Scripture, prayer, and my church community, the more I loved him (Upward). As I began to love him more, I began to love myself more—not in a narcissistic, self-centered way. I began to love myself because Jesus loved me and died for me. He thought I was worth the hell he experienced on the cross. If Jesus loved me that much, how could I not love myself? I began to see myself as God sees me. All that is true of Jesus was true of me. Because of him, and him alone, his Father became my Father. He loved me with an unfailing, never-giving-up-or-walking-out-on-you kind of love. I was forgiven of all my filth, and my sin was thrown into the sea of God's forgotten memory. I was now holy and blameless. My guilt was washed away by waves of grace. My shame was nailed to the cross, and my filthy rags of unrighteousness were exchanged for his robe of righteousness. His mercy triumphed judgment.

As I began to love God and myself correctly, the cage that locked my heart away in a cold, dark place was opened. I began to open myself up to loving others (Outward). I began to risk being hurt for the sake of loving people the way God loved me. One of the ways this newfound openness began to flesh out meant that I would become a pastor. It meant that I would surrender my fear of public speaking to God. It meant that I would offer my stuttering problem to God as an act of worship. It meant that I would trust him to transform a source of pain into a source of blessing—and he did. And he will do it for you too.

People who are progressively growing in loving God, self, and neighbor experience the God-kind-of-happiness.

Blessed

Perhaps at this point, you're thinking to yourself, *Derwin, I'm feeling what you are saying. But, as I read the Beatitudes, I don't see anything about happiness. The Scripture says "blessed," not "happy."* Great observation!

In the Old Testament, the Hebrew word for *blessed* is *ašerê*, which means to be in a state of happiness.[13] In the New Testament, the Greek word for *blessed* is *makários,* and it also means to be in a state of happiness.[14] Dallas Willard insightfully wrote that *makários* "refers to the highest type of well-being possible for human beings, but it is also the term the Greeks used for the kind of blissful existence characteristic of the gods."[15] The original readers of the Gospel of Matthew, where we find the Beatitudes, would have been aware of what *makários* meant. He was inviting people to be happy.

And he is still inviting people to be happy.

According to Jesus, the blessed, or happy, are those whose lives are supernaturally interwoven into Jesus' life, and who are participating in his kingdom by the Holy Spirit's power. C. S. Lewis turns the light up a little brighter for us to see:

> The happiness which God designs for His higher creatures is the happiness of being freely, voluntarily united to him and to each other in an ecstasy of love and delight compared with which the most rapturous love between a man and woman in this earth is mere milk and water.[16]

The happiness of God's kingdom is not about perpetually feeling good or good things consistently happening to us. The God-kind-of-happiness expressed in the Beatitudes is about *being* good and *becoming* a person who images forth the character of Jesus into the world by the power of the Holy Spirit.[17] If you will, Jesus makes us good by imparting and implanting his good life into us, utterly transforming our being.

We are reborn, recreated after our Creator.

We literally become a new creation.

We move from darkness to light, death to life.

The deeper we immerse ourselves in Jesus and his kingdom, the more we are supernaturally sculpted into his image, and the happier we will become.

How do we become more like Jesus? Like the disciples, we sit at his feet to learn. The New Testament uses the term *Christian* only three times to describe Jesus' followers. The term used most to describe Jesus' followers is *disciple*. It's used 269 times. In the first-century, Second Temple Jewish world of Jesus, a disciple was the student of a rabbi. The students' task was to follow and observe the rabbi, to learn at his feet, and then to pattern their lives after his. Jesus is our rabbi, and we are to observe him through the Scriptures, to learn at his feet and through the life of a local church, and then to *allow him to live his life* through us by faith. The good life, the happy life, is a life of discipleship.

. . . .

THE DEEPER WE IMMERSE OURSELVES IN JESUS AND HIS KINGDOM, THE MORE WE ARE SUPERNATURALLY SCULPTED INTO HIS IMAGE, AND THE HAPPIER WE WILL BECOME.

. . . .

The good life that we desire and, more important, we were created for, is available to us.

Two thousand years ago, on a hill over the Sea of Galilee, our good King invited us to discover the happiness we long to experience. The invitation still stands. You don't have to chase shadows anymore. Jesus—happiness himself—is chasing you.

Are you ready?

———————————— Marinate on This ————————————

Prayer

Father,

I'm discovering that life is exhilarating, messy,
beautiful, and perplexing.

I seem to have a longing that no created thing
can satisfy. Just when I think I'm going to
be happy for longer than just a few fleeting
moments, I realize I'm back where I started,
chasing something that seems to be uncatchable.

King Jesus,

I heard rumors that you have the key that
unlocks the door to happiness.

I heard that the happiness of God's kingdom
is not about perpetually feeling good or good
things consistently happening to me. The God-
kind-of-happiness expressed in the Beatitudes is
about me *being* good and *becoming* a person who
images forth your character into the world by the
power of the Holy Spirit.

Holy Spirit,

Thank you for imparting and implanting Jesus'
good life into me. I am in him and he is in me.
May he live his good life through me, for his
glory and my happiness.

In Jesus' name, amen.

Questions for Reflection

1. Take some time to reflect on "the pursuit of happiness." How have you pursued happiness in your life? Has it been fruitful? Have there been pitfalls?

2. Jesus was the happiest person ever to live. What made him happy?

3. Have you always imagined Jesus as happy, or are you surprised to learn that? Is it hard to believe Jesus was happy, even on the cross? How was he able to find happiness even in a terrible and torturous situation?

4. Reflect on the concept of Upward, Inward, Outward. How does it change your view of the good life?

5. Read Matthew 5:1–12. As you read through these verses, what surprises you?

6. True happiness comes from becoming a person who images forth the character of Jesus into the world. What steps can you take this week to become more like Christ?

Things to Remember

1. We can look to Jesus as the ultimate example of happiness because happiness is found in becoming a person who images forth the character of Jesus into the world.

2. The pursuit of the good life will you let down, but the pursuit of the God life will lead to joy.

3. The happiness of God's kingdom is not about perpetually feeling good; it's about the happiness expressed in the Beatitudes, which helps us become like Christ.

4. Jesus' circumstances were the window through which he expressed his happiness; they were not the cause of his happiness. Our circumstances do not add or take away from our happiness.

5. The deeper we immerse ourselves in Jesus and his kingdom, the more we are sculpted into his image, and the happier we will become.

CHAPTER 2

Happy Are the Beggars

"Blessed are the poor in spirit, for the kingdom of heaven is theirs." (Matthew 5:3)

Have you ever seen a beggar panhandling on a street corner? Perhaps the person begging looked worn and weary. Their clothes were scruffy and dirty. Without speaking a word, you could see that life has been hard for them. When I see people panhandling, I often wonder what happened in their lives that landed them here.

From a spiritual perspective, despite our money, clothes, homes, vehicles, and jobs, we are all beggars in need of God's grace. It's as if we were standing on the street corner of life—weary, worn, and battered. We are spiritually bankrupt. We have an eternal debt that we can never pay. No matter how hard we work, our bank account reads, "Insufficient funds."

But here's the good news. One day, Jesus shows up on the street corner that we beg on and offers us riches beyond belief. He offers not only to pay the debt that we owe, but to grant us an infinite, unending credit line to his Father. We now have everything we need and more.

But the riches that he offers are not what we expect. In fact, they are different than anything we've ever heard.

Our souls hunger for bread; Jesus offers us himself, the Bread of Life.

Our naked souls are ashamed; Jesus offers to clothe us with himself, covering our shame.

As we beg standing in our dirty clothes, Jesus offers to clothe us in his robe of righteousness.

Our souls need a home; as we wander the streets homeless, Jesus offers us his kingdom as our new home, his people as our new family.

Jesus tells us to lose ourselves in order to find our lives.

He tells us that only beggars can experience the riches of grace.

Only the poor in spirit—that is, spiritual beggars—are welcome in the King's kingdom. At the entrance to Jesus' kingdom is a sign that reads, "Only beggars past this point."

An ancient Jewish song says, "This poor man cried, and the LORD heard him and saved him from all his troubles" (Ps. 34:6). The word *poor* in Hebrew can be translated "humble." God is attracted to the humble or poor in spirit. He loves to rescue those who cry out to him in need. Just as a baby's journey to adulthood begins with a cry, our journey to happiness begins as a cry. We cry out because our worst moment and best moment occur simultaneously in the recognition that we are utterly spiritually bankrupt, and that God is utterly rich in mercy. God's mercy meets our need.

> But God, who is rich in mercy, because of his
> great love that he had for us, made us alive with

Christ even though we were dead in trespasses.
You are saved by grace! (Eph. 2:4–5)

Just as oil and water don't mix, God's grace and our pride do not mix. Pride keeps us blind to our need for grace. It keeps us self-reliant and resistant to God's grace. Only a heart emptied of pride can be filled with grace.

> But when the kindness of God our Savior and his love for mankind appeared, he saved us—not by works of righteousness that we had done, but according to his mercy—through the washing of regeneration and renewal by the Holy Spirit. He poured out his Spirit on us abundantly through Jesus Christ our Savior so that, having been justified by his grace, we may become heirs with the hope of eternal life. (Titus 3:4–7)

Pride

Pride is sneaky. It's like a deadly parasite that creeps up on an unsuspecting host, where it lives unnoticed before leading to sickness. As I think about it, as a younger man I had pride in my humility. I was proud that I didn't brag like other people or that I was humbler than them. I would brag about my humility. How ironic! I've now discovered that humility is like beauty; when you are beautiful, you don't have to tell anyone. They will just notice.

I was proud of being the first in my family to attend college. I was proud that I had never been arrested. I was proud that I didn't have any children outside of marriage. I was proud that I didn't have a substance abuse problem. I was proud of how hard I worked to earn a football scholarship. I was proud that I made it to the NFL. I was a proud man.

On the surface, the accomplishments that I was proud of were good things. I was living the American Dream, the good life. Little did I know that I was seriously infected by pride.

Here's the danger: I was self-sufficient and self-dependent. I was my own god. People who are self-sufficient and self-dependent justify and minimize their shortcomings while highlighting other people's shortcomings to feel better about themselves. I was so busy looking at the twigs in everyone else's eyes, I couldn't see the giant sequoia in my own.

Being poor in spirit means to see your spiritual bankruptcy so that you can make room for the treasures of Christ. The problem with pride is that even our good actions are tainted by our self-righteousness. In the early 1990s, my wife and I started the Derwin Gray Foundation to provide college scholarships for at-risk youth who were in under-resourced communities. We also provided about fifty tickets to Indianapolis Colts home games for kids who fit the same demographic. In the old RCA Dome, there was a massive banner with the words, "The Gray Zone." Every time I looked up at those kids sitting in The Gray Zone, pride gripped me. I thought to myself, *Look at how nice I am helping these poor kids.* For goodness' sake, Mayor Stephen Goldsmith even named October 14, 1996, "Derwin Gray Day" for my outstanding community service!

Once again, on the surface, this was a good thing. But underneath the surface, where we truly live, my heart took a good thing and made it a god thing because I was the hero of the story.

I've now come to learn that Jesus is a King who does not share his glory with anyone. He is a King who created us for worship—that is, to find our love, significance, identity, and purpose in him. He is a King who knows that we become like what we worship, so he created us to worship him, so we could become like him. Our EGO, which stands for *Edging God Out*,[1] tries to make us the center of the story, but Jesus, in his faithful, unending love, doesn't want us to *dehumanize ourselves* by worshiping false gods. It's not that he *needs* us to worship him. God doesn't need anything. But he made us in such a way that true happiness can only be found when we worship him. When we worship ourselves, we will only find emptiness at the end of it all.

I was ruining myself because I was worshiping myself.

In Need of Rescue

A prideful man can never see God because he's too preoccupied with the reflection staring at him in the mirror. A prideful man is the sun, and everyone revolves around him—so he thinks.

I was perhaps the worst kind of prideful man. I was the prideful man who thought he was humble and good. People who think they are not full of pride can't see the King who only rescues those who are humble enough to ask for rescuing.

For example, while on vacation in Western Montana, where my wife is from, I once did something I still can't believe. While attempting to water ski, and after I had fallen for the millionth time, I told my father-in-law, who was driving the boat, "Leave me in the water. I'm going to dog-paddle back to the shore." *I can't even swim!* Somehow, in my mind, I decided that I was going to dog-paddle about four hundred yards back to the shore in a massive lake. About thirty seconds into this brilliant idea, I realized that the harder I attempted to swim, the more the currents took me further from the shore. Panic began to seize my body as I then realized that a boat, moving at a high rate of speed, was heading toward me. I tried to dive underwater, but I couldn't because I had on a life preserver. Thankfully, the boat narrowly missed me. After several minutes of drifting away and getting more fatigued, my father-in-law came back to rescue me.

This was easily one of the dumbest and most dangerous things I've ever done. But that's what pride does. It lands you in need of rescue, because it makes you over-confident and over-reliant on yourself. We were created to be completely confident and completely reliant on God. It is only in our weakness that God shares his strength with us.

The Birthplace of All Sin

Pride is the mother of all sin because it gives birth to every other sin. The word *sin* literally means "to miss the mark." In the ancient world, when an archer would shoot his arrow at the target, aiming for the bull's-eye, if he missed it, the judge would say, "Sin." It was sin because the archer missed the mark.

Similarly, God created us to live in a certain way—kind of like archers shooting arrows that cultivate his kingdom on earth. It is sin when we choose to shoot arrows at the target of our kingdoms instead of his. Instead of being God's archers, we become God's enemies with agendas that compete with his. Instead of partnering with God, we have partnered with dark powers that oppose him.

But how did this happen? Has it always been this way? Let's start at the beginning: all of humanity is made in God's image.

In the ancient world, a king would place statues of himself throughout his kingdom, so the citizens would know who the king was and whom they served. The God of heaven and earth does the same thing: Adam, Eve, and all their children were made to be image-bearers throughout creation, displaying God's glory, goodness, and wisdom.

> You made him [man] little less than God and crowned him with glory and honor. You made him ruler over the works of your hands; you put everything under his feet. . . . LORD, our Lord, how magnificent is your name throughout the earth! (Ps. 8:5–6, 9)

God's image-bearers were to multiply and populate the earth with his image by living lives of confidence and reliance on him. The environment of heaven was to cover the earth through their partnership with God. In fact, earth was to be a mini-version of God's realm. The garden of Eden was God's temple, and Adam, Eve, and their offspring were to be God's living statues, functioning as his priests. As they bore children and multiplied God's image, the temple-garden would spread to cover all of creation, and God's kingdom reign would cover everything that existed. Adam and Eve were animated when God breathed divine life into them and sustained this life with the tree of life (Gen. 2:7, 9). As Adam and Eve ate from the tree of life, they showed their confidence and reliance on God himself. He was their source and purpose. He promised to sustain their life and give them purpose, and they promised to obey

God by relying on him, cultivating the garden, and multiplying his image.

Now, imagine with me for a moment that your father is the greatest king and ruler on earth. You are his little girl—the apple of his eye. His love toward you is extravagant, and your every need is met by his gracious hand. Your role in his kingdom is clear: you are to represent him to all of creation. Your only covenant obligation is to trust and rely on your father's love, wisdom, and strength.

But one day, a high-ranking, disgruntled general in your father's kingdom comes to you and says, "Let me ask you a question. Are you sure your father has your best interests in mind? Why should you have to use *your* life to push his agenda? What about *your* agenda? What about what *you* want? You know, I've been observing you since you were a little girl. You have great ideas, you have great vision, you have great ability. Why should your father get all the glory when you are doing all the work? It seems to me that your father never wants you to have your own kingdom because your kingdom could be greater than his. You are not a child any more. *It's time for you to live your life.* I'll even help you."

This story is not so much different than the one we read in Genesis 3. Satan lied to Adam and Eve, tempting them with a distorted vision of the good life. They were already living the good life, but he led them to believe God was holding out on them.

And that forked tongue still whispers the same lie to us.

God created his children to be like him, but the only way they could be like him was to rely on him, not to oppose him by living independent from him. When Adam and Eve chose to become "like God, knowing good and evil" (Gen. 3:5), hell flooded earth, and has been drowning humanity ever since. Every hurt, every pain, every ugly form of human behavior had its origin in the garden.

> Therefore, just as sin entered the world through one man, and death through sin, in this way death spread to all people, because all sinned. (Rom. 5:12)

Adam and Eve's eating from the tree of the knowledge of good and evil was an act of rebellion. It was the most vicious form of pride, saying, "God, *I don't need you.*"

Sin is so much more than "I did something bad." Sin is renouncing our birthright to reign in God's kingdom for the sake of pursuing our own pitiful little kingdoms. Darkness entered the world when humanity failed to realize that the good life was already theirs, placed at their fingertips by God. They abandoned the glory of truly being like God—made in his likeness—because they wanted to be God. Tempted by an animal over

WHEN ADAM AND EVE CHOSE TO BECOME "LIKE GOD, KNOWING GOOD AND EVIL," HELL FLOODED EARTH, AND HAS BEEN DROWNING HUMANITY EVER SINCE.

whom they should have had dominion, they became like animals. We can't be poor in spirit when we are seeking to rule ourselves. We can't live the good life when we are wrapped up in our sinfulness. Instead of ruling with God, we are now ruled by sin, death, and the powers of evil. Adam and Eve chose slavery over freedom, and now we are born into slavery, in need of rescuing. We need to be restored to the good life God designed for us.

Since by the one man's trespass, death reigned through that one man, how much more will those who receive the overflow of grace and the gift of righteousness reign in life through the one man, Jesus Christ. (Rom. 5:17)

My Night Turned into Day

The night I came face-to-face with my pride was after a football game in 1995. Our team was making a push toward the playoffs, but first, we needed to beat the New Orleans Saints. In the first half of the game, I played well. But in the second half, I was called for two penalties that contributed to the Saints' coming back to beat us. I took the loss hard.

Upon our return to Indianapolis, my teammates and I went to a restaurant where I proceeded to get drunk. Now that I look back, I know I was self-medicating because I didn't want to face reality. My pride would not allow me to, so I threw myself a pity party. I was overwhelmed at the thought that I could lose my job. I thought if I lost my job as a football player, I would lose myself as a person. This thought was too much to bear.

During this same time, my wife was pregnant with our first child. During pregnancy, she suffered from a condition called *hyperemesis gravidarum,* which meant she vomited all day, every day. When I got home, a teammate carried me into the house. I stumbled toward our bedroom. When I opened the door, my pregnant, sick wife asked me, "Where have you been?" As I attempted to speak, projectile vomit sprayed from my mouth. I immediately fell to the ground and started groveling in the mess. I was incoherently saying, "I let the team down. I let the baby down. I let everybody down. I'm going to lose my job." Vicki and her older sister, who was in town to help take care of her, cleaned up as I lay passed out on the bed.

The next morning, I looked in the mirror and saw who I really was, a pride-filled, broken, weak man. I thought to myself, *Something is wrong with you.* I was starting to hit rock bottom. I wasn't quite there yet, but I was on my way.

Over the next two years, God graciously and sovereignly allowed the circumstances of life to peel the layers of my pride. My body began to break down, and when a football player's body fails him, his career is ending. Who would I be without the game? *I'd be a useless nobody*, I thought. I didn't love my wife the way she deserved. I couldn't love her because I didn't love God or myself. I also began to realize that I wasn't a good person like I had always thought. As Steve Grant, my Colts teammate (a.k.a. "The Naked Preacher"), communicated the gospel with me, he asked me to read Jesus' words, "No one is good except God alone" (Mark 10:18). The Holy Spirit used this Scripture to cut me deeply.

Before God could heal me, he had to humble me. I had to see my spiritual poverty and let go of my perceived right to rule.

Just like the cross of Christ, out of humility and hurt came help and healing. In comparison to God and his goodness, my pride was shattered, my sin was acknowledged, and my heart was open to his grace.

> But he gives greater grace. Therefore he says: God
> resists the proud, but gives grace to the humble.
> (James 4:6)

The house of cards that I had built my life on was blown down by the pursuing winds of God's love. It was only by recognizing that I was not good that I could experience the goodness of God. It was even the goodness of God that opened my eyes to see my need of his grace. I hit rock bottom and discovered that Jesus was the Rock.

On August 2, 1997, I met King Jesus, and I trusted him. With arms wide open, he welcomed me into his kingdom. I was now beginning my journey to understanding his life-giving words: "Blessed are the poor in spirit, for the kingdom of heaven is theirs" (Matt. 5:3).

This Greek word translated *poor* (*ptōchós*) was commonly used to describe a beggar who was dependent on a provider. In the Old Testament, the word implied hope in God alone.[2] Jesus is teaching us that the good life is only for beggars. Only for those completely dependent on God to provide every single thing we have. Only for those who hope in him alone.

Eighteenth-century hymn writer Augustus Toplady was right when he wrote, "Nothing in my hands I bring, Simply to Thy cross I cling."

Happy are the beggars for only they receive the unending riches of Christ.

> For you know the grace of our Lord Jesus Christ: Though he was rich, for your sake he became poor, so that by his poverty you might become rich. (2 Cor. 8:9)

Messianic Expectations

I never would have imagined that one day I would find myself standing where Jesus of Nazareth taught humanity how to be happy. While in Israel working on my doctorate, I visited the site where Jesus preached the Sermon on the Mount.

> When he saw the crowds, he went up on the mountain, and after he sat down, his disciples came to him. Then he began to teach them. . . .
> (Matt. 5:1–2)

As Jesus went up the hill to teach, his disciples sat at his feet, which was the common posture of disciples in the first-century Jewish world. Jesus still invites and wants his disciples to sit at his feet and learn.

The world of Jesus was pregnant with messianic expecta- tions. For centuries, the Jewish people awaited the arrival of the "Anointed One" or the Messiah (Christ). The Messiah would be born in Bethlehem (Micah 5:2); Jesus was born in Bethlehem (Matt. 2:1–2); He would be born of a virgin (Isa. 7:14); Jesus was born of a virgin (Matt. 1:22–23). The Messiah would crush the serpent (Gen. 3:15); Jesus did indeed crush the serpent through his redemptive work (Matt. 16:18; Rom. 16:20). He would be a bless- ing to every ethnic group on earth (Gen. 22:18), Jesus blesses and creates a family on earth comprised of all the families on earth, called the church (Gal. 3:16; Rev. 5:9–12). He would be the root and offspring of King David, from the royal line of Judah (2 Sam. 7:12); Jesus was a descendant of David, in the royal line of Judah (Acts 2:30). The Messiah would be a son, a child, and a king who sat on the throne of David forever (Isa. 9:6–7); Jesus is the son, the child, the King of the Jews who sits on the throne of David forever (Acts 2:34–36). Just as the prophet Isaiah proclaimed, the Messiah would be "pierced because of our rebellion, crushed because of our iniquities; punishment for our peace was on him, and we are healed by his wounds" (Isa. 53:5). Jesus is the Messiah. He is God's means of ushering in peace between God and humanity. He is the healer.

Like the Samaritan woman at the well, we say, "I know that the Messiah is coming" (who is called Christ). "When he comes, he will explain everything to us" (John 4:25), and Jesus says, "I, the one speaking to you, am he" (John 4:26).

As Jesus taught, the various groups of Jews, such as the Zealots, the Pharisees, the Sadducees, and the Essenes, would most likely have been listening to his sermons. They would have been on tip-toe awaiting God's promised Messiah, who would bring about a new exodus and set the Jewish people free from the tyranny of Rome. They were looking for a liberator. He was in their midst, but they didn't know it, because he was different than they expected.

One typical Saturday morning in Jesus' hometown of Nazareth, and like he had so many times before, Jesus went to the synagogue for worship, fellowship, prayer, and instruction. But then something unusual happened. Jesus was given the scroll of the prophet Isaiah, and he read:

> "The Spirit of the Lord is on me, because he has anointed me to preach good news to the poor. He has sent me to proclaim release to the captives and recovery of sight to the blind, to set free

the oppressed, to proclaim the year of the Lord's favor." (Luke 4:18–19)

After he was done reading, Jesus blew every listener's mind: "Today as you listen, this Scripture has been fulfilled" (Luke 4:21). Jesus was announcing that God's Messiah had come and that he was that Messiah. As Israel's Messiah, Jesus was the living portrait of the words he read. He ministered to the spiritually and materially poor; he set the demon-possessed free from dark powers; he gave sight to the blind, both physically and spiritually; he freed oppressed people from the power of sin and death; and he was the ultimate expression of Jubilee. In ancient Israel, every fifty years, the Year of Jubilee was to be celebrated. This meant all debt was forgiven, and property was restored (Lev. 25). Jesus is the new and better Jubilee, because he forgives all our sin-debt and restores us as God's sacred possession and royal priests.

If you are like most Americans, you have some form of debt. Debt can be crippling. Can you imagine someone paying off your college, credit card, and home mortgage debt all at once? Imagine how happy you'd be. Happy are those who let God pay off their sin-debt.

> He erased the certificate of debt, with its obligations, that was against us and opposed to us, and has taken it away by nailing it to the cross. (Col. 2:14)

> How joyful is the one whose transgression is forgiven, whose sin is covered! (Ps. 32:1)

Poor People Matter to Jesus

We've learned that Jesus' kingdom is only for beggars who recognize their need for his grace. In a beautiful irony, the book of Matthew was written by a rich man originally named Levi, but it wasn't until he became a poor beggar that he could experience the boundless riches of Christ (Mark 2:14). In the first-century Jewish world, a tax collector was the worst of the worst in the social order. Matthew/Levi was a pariah. He betrayed his kinsmen the Jews by taking a job with their oppressors, the brutal Roman Empire. He took tax money from them and gave it to the Romans—but not without first overcharging them and skimming some money off the top to make himself rich. As a tax collector, Matthew most likely would not have been welcomed in the synagogue. Yet Jesus invited a man like Matthew into his kingdom. A respectable rabbi would never want a tax collector as a disciple. But Jesus is not your everyday rabbi; he specializes in calling the marginalized, the poor, the lowly, the beggars.

JESUS SPECIALIZES IN CALLING THE MARGINALIZED, THE POOR, THE LOWLY, THE BEGGARS.

Jesus was himself among the *Anawim*, a group of economically underprivileged Jews.[3] Many Jewish historians agree that the *Anawim* were economically poor, but they were God-reliant. The temple was their meeting place, and they were characterized by a deep longing for the Messiah's advent, so he could bring about justice, righting all the wrongs.[4]

There is a special something that I can only describe as a beautiful, inspiring grace-gift that the poor who are God-reliant have. A few years ago, in the slums of Kolkata, India, I encountered some of the happiest, godliest, and most beautiful people I had ever met. These precious disciples of Jesus converted a garbage dump into their living community. What they lacked in money and possessions, they made up for with the God-kind-of-happiness that money can't buy. The little church in this community taught the women and men skills to get jobs and educate the children. It was a stunning picture of holistic discipleship. I thought I was going to the slums of Kolkata to help these poor people; upon my return to America, I realized that I was poor and that they, out of their spiritual abundance, helped me far more than I helped them.

There are more than two thousand verses in the Bible about the poor. Don't move too fast. Slow down and marinate on this for a moment. God loves the poor, and so should we. Unfortunately, and to the detriment of the church, it seems like some Christians blame the poor for being poor. It's like the poor must have done something wrong because "this is America, and everyone can and should pull themselves up by their bootstraps. Otherwise, they must be lazy and irresponsible." There is some truth to that statement, but it's not all-the-way true. Yes, some people are lazy. Yes, some people are irresponsible. But it is also important to acknowledge that the scales of justice in our great country have not been equally balanced. In a land where women could not vote until 1920, where black Americans were enslaved and later attacked by police dogs simply for wanting to exercise their American right to vote, where Native Americans have experienced genocide, and where poor whites in Appalachia have been left behind, some people have benefited more than others. Some people have more access to the tools necessary to "pull yourself up by your bootstraps" than others. It's like playing

Monopoly, but passing "Go" three times, buying the best properties, and collecting the most money before the other players start, and then wondering why you won the game. The game was set up for you to win!

As followers of Jesus, we are called to "remember the poor" as the early church asked the apostle Paul (Gal. 2:10). When we bless the poor, we are blessing God.

> Kindness to the poor is a loan to the LORD, and
> he will give a reward to the lender. (Prov. 19:17)

> The one who gives to the poor will not be in need,
> but one who turns his eyes away will receive many
> curses. (Prov. 28:27)

The book of James was written by the half-brother of Jesus to first-century Jewish congregations where wealthy members of the church were exploiting the poor members (James 5:1–6), showing favoritism to the wealthy over the poor (James 2:1–4, 9), and neglecting to meet the needs of the poor (James 2:15–16). As *Anawim* himself, James challenged the rich to love their siblings in Christ. He said that how you care for your poor brothers and sisters is a reflection of your love for God:

> Indeed, if you fulfill the royal law prescribed in
> the Scripture, Love your neighbor as yourself, you
> are doing well. (James 2:8)

James explored what it looks like to be a citizen of God's kingdom: "Pure and undefiled religion before God the Father is this: to look after orphans and widows in their distress and to keep oneself unstained from the world" (James 1:27). True worship is not merely what we say we believe, but how we love our neighbor, especially the most vulnerable in our community.

In the first-century Greco-Roman world, widows and orphans were the most vulnerable. James' words evoke the prophet Ezekiel's words, "Father and mother are treated with contempt, and the resident alien is exploited within you. The fatherless and widow are oppressed in you" (Ezek. 22:7). If a brother or sister in Christ lacks clothes or food and you meet their need, you have a "living faith" according to James (2:14–17). Just as Jesus loved and cared for the poor in his earthly ministry, as brothers and sisters in the Messiah, we are to love and care for the poor in the church family as well as those outside church:

> Instruct those who are rich in the present age not to be arrogant or to set their hope on the uncertainty of wealth, but on God, who richly provides us with all things to enjoy. Instruct them to do what is good, to be rich in good works, to be generous and willing to share, storing up treasure for themselves as a good foundation for the coming age, so that they may take hold of what is truly life. (1 Tim. 6:17–19)

How we treat the poor reflects our nearness to God. Just as we were spiritually poor and Jesus met our need with the abundance of his grace, as God's people we are to draw near the poor and meet their needs with our abundance.

Not only do we meet the need of physical poverty, but of spiritual poverty as well. We feed hungry hearts and hungry stomachs.

Just as Jesus fed the hungry in his ministry and died on the cross for sins, we, too, are called into the world to meet both physical and spiritual needs. This is the good life.

Happy are those who declare spiritual bankruptcy, for only then can the riches of Christ fill the bank vault of their hearts with his love and kingdom.

HOW WE TREAT THE POOR REFLECTS OUR NEARNESS TO GOD.

——————————— Marinate on This ———————————

Prayer

Holy Spirit,

Would you grant me the spiritual eyes to see my
true condition outside of Jesus?

I do not have the capacity to see my need of
grace with my own ability.

Open the eyes of my heart that I may see that
your mercy met my need.

Father,

Thank you for sending your beloved Son.
Though he was rich, he became poor for my
sake, so I could inherit his wealth.

All that I have and all that I am is because he is
the Great I Am.

Lord Jesus,

Considering your abundant grace toward me,
may I love the poor the way you love the poor.

In response to your love, may I care for the
vulnerable the way you care for the vulnerable.

May the least of these see the greatest of these—
you—in and through my life.

In Jesus' name, amen.

Questions for Reflection

1. This chapter focuses on Matthew 5:3. Take some time to pray and meditate on this verse. How has your understanding of "poor in spirit" changed after reading this chapter?

2. Pride is sneaky. In my own experience, I took great pride in being humble (and didn't realize what an oxymoron that is). How have you struggled with pride and humility? Can you think of a time when pride snuck up on you?

3. Read 2 Corinthians 8:9. How did Jesus display humility?

4. Pride blinds us to our need for grace. How can you submit your pride to God and replace it with humility? What steps can you take to see God's grace more clearly?

5. Have you ever had an experience where someone paid a debt that you owed? How did you feel? Do you recall when you fully comprehended that God paid your sin-debt? How does it make you feel to know that he has? What is your response?

6. What can you do this week to love the poor and marginalized in your community? Take steps toward being a holistic healer; this is the good life.

Things to Remember

1. Being poor in spirit means that you see and accept your spiritual bankruptcy so that you can make room for the treasures of Christ.

2. We were created to be completely confident and completely reliant on God. It is only in our weakness that God shares his strength with us.

3. When you hit rock bottom, remember that Jesus is the Rock.

4. We can't be poor in spirit when we are seeking to rule ourselves. We can't live the good life when we're wrapped up in our sinfulness.

5. Just like the cross of Christ, out of humility and hurt come help and healing.

CHAPTER 3

Happy Are the Sad

"Blessed are those who mourn,
for they will be comforted." (Matthew 5:4)

A s Jesus continued to teach, with his disciples sitting at his feet, Matthew recorded him saying, "Blessed are those who mourn, for they will be comforted" (Matt. 5:4). Jesus used the Greek word *pentheō* (mourn). *Pentheō* is the strongest word for mourning or lamenting in the New Testament.[1] It expresses loud crying, as if someone is wailing in agony over sin, suffering, injustice, and human tragedy. It describes a person whose heart is broken by what breaks God's heart.

Over the years of sitting at Jesus' feet, I've found that the more time I spend with him, the more I am connected to his heart. And somehow, in a way that only he understands, I am a better person because my love for people and their plight increases.

Lamenting is a holy hurt. But the hurt is a pain that pushes us deeper into faith, hope, and love.

Deeper in my faith in Jesus and his redemptive purposes.

Deeper into hoping, *which is a knowing* that one day all things will be made new.

Deeper into loving people.

In the midst of human suffering, having someone who cares for you, comforts you, prays with you, reads Scripture over you, and nurtures you through the rising river of pain is a gift. It's as if God heals us as we become instruments of healing touch.

Those who lament will be cemented in God's comfort. God's comforting grace will be experienced in the present through the Spirit's presence, and in the future, when ultimate redemption is realized in the new heavens and new earth. Just like the cross, out of great sorrow comes great comfort. Happy are those whose hearts break for what breaks God's heart, for they will be comforted.

. . . .
**LAMENTING IS A
HOLY HURT.**
. . . .

I want to introduce you to a few people who have learned to lament in the midst of life's pain.

Abigail

Abigail grew up as a pastor's kid following the Christian script: she loved Jesus, she loved her parents, she served in her dad's church, and she even shared her faith with others. After graduation from high school, the plan was to head off to a good Christian school, where she'd meet a good Christian man, graduate, get married, get a career, and then have some good Christian kids.

One day during Abigail's freshman year in college, she felt a pain so intense that it knocked her back and took her breath away. The pain was devastating, like nothing she had ever experienced. One doctor visit turned into many, each more frustrating than the last. Her physical condition got worse, and her pain turned into chronic pain. Eventually, Abigail was diagnosed with chronic kidney stones and an incurable bladder disease.

Abigail has had as many as 240 kidney stones at one time! Her bladder disease is also painful. Her doctor explained to her that the medication that could help with the chronic kidney stones would make her bladder disease worse, and the medication for the bladder disease would make her chronic kidney stones worse. Abigail is a medical mystery. She's been to the top medical experts in America, and there is no relief in sight.

As weeks turned into months, Abigail began to grieve the life she hadn't even begun to live. She grieved that she had to come home from college and would potentially never have a career. She grieved that she may never get married and have kids. She grieved that her life was going in reverse. Not only were the dark rain clouds of chronic pain pouring down on her, but the thunderstorms of depression and anxiety began to take up residence in her mind. She found herself constantly hurting physically, emotionally, and mentally. She isolated herself more and more. For two years, she only left her parents' home to go to the grocery store and to get her hair done. She felt like she was imprisoned in her own body and mind.

I wish I could tell you that this only lasted a little while, but I can't. For more than a decade, Abigail has lived in chronic pain. She stopped attending church. She felt abandoned by God, asking, "If Jesus has the power to heal me, why won't he?" In this season of doubt, her father would often tell her, "A troubled faith is better than no faith" and "A faith that is not tested is a faith that cannot be trusted."[2] These words eventually became a lifeline for Abigail.

Despite her grim circumstances, Abigail still wanted to give Jesus another chance. In 2016, she came across my book *Limitless*

Life: You Are More Than Your Past When God Holds Your Future.
The part of the book that God used most deeply was when I wrote
about my wife, Vicki, being diagnosed with thyroid cancer.

May 17, 2004 is a day forever tattooed in my soul because that's
the day the love of my life, my best friend, the greatest person I
know, and the mother of my children was diagnosed with thyroid
cancer. Vicki was a college track and field athlete and a registered
dietician. She exercised, ate right, and walked closely with Jesus, yet
cancer knocked on her door and became an uninvited guest. I can
still remember when the doctor told us, "You are not going to like
this news. Vicki, you have thyroid cancer." After he said the word
cancer, time stood still, and my body went numb.

No one tells you that the first night you or a loved one are
diagnosed with cancer, it's impossible to sleep. Thoughts of burying
my wife raced through my mind. Our kids, who at the time were
eight and four, could grow up without their momma. I was terrified.

By God's grace, through a skilled surgeon and radioactive
iodine, Vicki has been cancer-free since 2004. Cancer has left her
body, but what we learned about God has not. In *Limitless Life*, I
shared things we learned from Romans 5:3–5:

> And not only that, but we also rejoice in our
> afflictions, because we know that affliction pro-
> duces endurance, endurance produces proven
> character, and proven character produces hope.
> This hope will not disappoint us, because God's
> love has been poured out in our hearts through
> the Holy Spirit who was given to us.

First, we learned that God does not waste our pain. It's as though God takes our pain and uses it to purify us. Through our experience with Vicki's cancer, we learned suffering produces perseverance. During suffering, God graciously grants us access to the suffering of Christ Jesus. His endurance becomes ours. In our weakness, his strength becomes ours. I wrote:

> As fear marched around our minds like an invading army, we retreated deeper into Jesus. He became our fortress of hope. As we pressed into him, Jesus grew our roots deeper and deeper into the soil of his great love. This made us stronger. It made us tougher.[3]

Second, we learned that the endurance wrought by suffering leads to proven character. God's greatest goal, his unrelenting aim and passion, is to form Christ in us. Just like training an athlete, God, in his sovereign love, allows the brokenness of this world to be tools in his nail-pierced hands to heal our broken character. Through the flames of suffering, he forges our character to reflect Jesus' character:

> I never, ever want to go through cancer again. But as we journeyed through the valley of death, our attention to Jesus and to life was heightened. We saw the world differently: colors were brighter, food was better, people became more valuable, and our passion for reaching others with the gospel intensified. As we pressed into Jesus, his character became our character. What became

important to him became important to us. Our capacity to love and not sweat the small stuff increased exponentially.[4]

Third, we learned that proven character produces hope because the love of God is poured into our hearts. It's quite a mystery that suffering expands our capacity to understand how much God loves us. Perhaps in suffering, we get a glimpse of how Jesus suffered for the sins of the world. The only reason there is cancer, bladder disease, depression, anxiety, and other forms of pain is that creation itself is broken and longing to be rescued from decay and corruption. Creation is fallen and in need of redemption just like humanity is. The cross of Jesus will eventually even heal creation:

> **GOD'S GREATEST GOAL, HIS UNRELENTING AIM AND PASSION, IS TO FORM CHRIST IN US.**

> For I consider that the sufferings of this present time are not worth comparing with the glory that is going to be revealed to us. For the creation eagerly waits with anticipation for God's sons to be revealed. For the creation was subjected to futility—not willingly, but because of him who subjected it—in the hope that the creation itself will also be set free from the bondage to decay into the glorious freedom of God's children. For we know that the whole creation has been groaning together with labor pains until now. Not only that, but we ourselves who have the Spirit as

the firstfruits—we also groan within ourselves, eagerly waiting for adoption, the redemption of our bodies. Now in this hope we were saved, but hope that is seen is not hope, because who hopes for what he sees? Now if we hope for what we do not see, we eagerly wait for it with patience. (Rom. 8:18–25)

Hope has a name, and it's Jesus. Through his cross and resurrection, our bodies, along with all of creation, will be made whole. But until that time, God lovingly enters our suffering and is broken on a cross to heal our brokenness. Our hope is not a mere wish, but an assurance, because God through the Holy Spirit is pouring his love into our hearts.

> Happy is the one whose help is the God of Jacob,
> whose hope is in the LORD his God. (Ps. 146:5)

It was this section of *Limitless Life* that gripped Abigail's heart. A new script was being written for her. God is the author of the script, the producer, the director, and Abigail was the actor in this new divine drama. I'm sure she'd rather not play this role, but she is learning what it means to lament and trust God in her chronic pain. She is learning that God can use unfavorable situations to display his favor in her life. Lament is an ancient expression for mourning or grieving loss. As she began to lament her condition, God began to cement her deeper into his love:

> The LORD is near the brokenhearted; he saves those crushed in spirit. (Ps. 34:18)

Recently, Abigail shared her story at Transformation Church, the church I pastor. There was not a dry eye in the house, as God's Spirit moved powerfully. Out of a heart of lament, God began to shape people in his redemptive, character-forming love. God took the lament of pain that Vicki and I experienced through her cancer and used it to bring healing grace to Abigail. Then Abigail offered her lament to God, and he used it to spread his hope-giving love to the Transformation Church family. Here's an example:

> I felt lost and I desperately needed anything to find me and tell me that I belonged. Then a few days ago I started praying and asked God to help me. I asked him to help me find where I truly belonged, and the very next day my best friend texted me asking if I wanted to go to Transformation Church. It's been a little over a year since we've been, and that was the quickest "Yes" I've ever sent back.
>
> This is the service that I truly needed. I know that I'm not suffering like Abigail is, but I had gotten to a point that my faith was slowly starting to dim. But then she said, "A faith that has not been tested, cannot be trusted," and I knew right then and there that those words were God calling me back. I honestly felt like I belonged because I was able to witness someone else's faith be dimmed but then find her way back to him. I just wanted to tell anyone I could how blessed I felt to be there today. I feel good and whole. Thank you so much for today!

Happy are those who lament, for God cements them more firmly into his life-giving love.

Dwayne and Pam

I met Dwayne at a Transformation Church Newcomers event. This is a time for people new to Transformation Church to meet our staff and non-staff leaders. Dwayne had silver hair with a touch of an "I-used-to-wear-my-hair-like-Elvis" look. He was in his sixties and talked with a deep South Carolina drawl. Dwayne was as country as country can get.

He was also in mourning.

Pam, Dwayne's wife of more than thirty years, had had enough, and she had divorced him. She had been his world. He was there that day because he had heard about this new church in the community where old people, young people, black people, white people, Latino people, Asian people, rich people, and poor people gathered and listened to a preacher who used to play professional football. So he thought he'd give it a try.

I noticed Dwayne talking to some of our staff, so I walked over to introduce myself. Before he even spoke a word, sadness and grief colored his countenance. As Dwayne poured his heart out, he was lamenting that he was the primary cause of his divorce. He had attended church for years—that's kind of what you do in South Carolina—but he hadn't allowed Jesus to penetrate his insecurity, selfishness, and defensiveness. Dwayne attended church, but he hadn't allowed Jesus to develop him into a disciple.

After thirty years, Pam's soul couldn't bear the weight of his lack of repentance. I give Dwayne credit; as he talked to me that night, he didn't blame Pam at all for the divorce. He owned his sin. He lamented his sin. And God's comfort was on its way.

But it would take time.

I told Dwayne that the Lord could reconcile his marriage, but it began with letting Jesus heal and transform him. He bought in. He faithfully attended worship every Sunday, sought counseling, and began to develop rhythms of grace like Scripture study, prayer, connecting in a small group, and serving the body of Christ. As I preached on Sundays, I began to notice a woman sitting next to him. She looked cold and distant, but as the weeks turned into months, her cold exterior melted, and they began to hold hands.

Soon, Pam and Dwayne started attending marriage counseling together, resulting in Dwayne and Pam telling me that they wanted to get remarried, and they did. Dwayne and Pam are trophies of God's grace; they are the personification of how lament will cement us deeper into God's soul-healing grace.

Often, we think loss and grief distance us from God, but the reality is that God is near those who mourn their sin because then, and only then, does his grace flood in. I asked Dwayne and Pam to share their story at Transformation Church. Out of their mourning, not only were they comforted, but the Spirit of God used their story as a means of comforting others in a similar circumstance.

The first time I met Dwayne, he was a sad man. All that has changed now. His face beams with happiness:

> Those who look to him are radiant with joy; their
> faces will never be ashamed. (Ps. 34:5)

Bryan

Author and lawyer Bryan Stevenson grew up on the eastern shore of Delmarva Peninsula, Delaware. His community was rural, poor, and racially segregated. Some people he knew didn't even have indoor plumbing. His community was "unapologetically Southern."[5]

Despite being in Delaware, he writes, "Confederate flags were proudly displayed throughout the region, boldly and definitely marking the cultural, social, and political landscape."[6]

Despite his economic disadvantages, Bryan willed his way through hard work, discipline, and intellectual genius to Harvard Law. In 1983, as a twenty-three-year-old student, he signed up for an internship in Georgia. This internship would transform his life and literally save the lives of people who have been marginalized and discounted.

Bryan didn't want to become a lawyer, but he didn't know what to do with his life. He had a desire to help the poor, to heal America's racial inequality, and to assist in making America equitable and fair.[7] I suspect Bryan's upbringing shaped his heart to alleviate suffering. The things he witnessed and experienced caused him to lament, and his lament caused him to do something.

During his search for his life's plan, the plan found him. He learned that Harvard Law offered a one-month, intensive, boots-on-the-ground course on race and poverty litigation.[8] This piqued his attention, especially since it was taught by Betsy Bartholet, a law professor who had worked as an attorney with the NAACP legal defense fund.[9] Bryan was excited because this course would take him off-campus. He would be required to spend a month with the Southern Prisoners Defense Committee (SPDC) doing justice work.[10]

On his flight to Atlanta to spend a few weeks working with the SPDC, Bryan met Steve Bright, the director of the SPDC! Steve told Bryan, "Capital punishment means 'them without the capital get the punishment.' We can't help people on death row without help from people like you."[11] This conversation was a game-changer for Bryan.

Isn't it amazing that one decision can make a difference in someone's life and affect generations? A decision is like a river that changes course. Bryan's choice to say "Yes" to the SPDC would eventually become a river of life for those condemned to death. As Bryan got close to people on death row, he wrote, "Proximity to the condemned and incarcerated made the question of each person's humanity more urgent and meaningful, including my own."[12]

In some ways, this is a picture of the incarnation of Jesus. The eternal Son of God became one of us. He got up close to us, condemned and incarcerated in the prison cell of sin, death, and evil. We have Jesus as our defense attorney. We couldn't afford him, so his Daddy gave him to us for free. Our defense attorney fights for our freedom. Every other attorney would lose our case because we are beyond-the-shadow-of-a-doubt guilty. Our defense attorney assumes our guilt, takes our sentence, and does our time, so we can be set free, exonerated from all of our crimes. As Bryan entered the world of those deemed fit to die on death row, he lamented:

> My work with the poor and incarcerated has persuaded me that the opposite of poverty is not wealth; the opposite of poverty is justice. Finally,

I've come to believe that the true measure of our commitment to justice, the character of our society, our commitment to the rule of law, fairness, and equality cannot be measured by how we treat the rich, the powerful, the privileged, and the respected among us. The true measure of our character is how we treat the poor, the disfavored, the accused, the incarcerated, the condemned. We are all implicated when we allow other people to be mistreated.[13]

Bryan's words have a similar ring to them as Jesus' words:

"Then they too will answer, 'Lord, when did we see you hungry, or thirsty, or a stranger, or without clothes, or sick, or in prison, and not help you?'

"Then he will answer them, 'Truly I tell you, whatever you did not do for one of the least of these, you did not do for me.'

"And they will go away into eternal punishment, but the righteous into eternal life." (Matt. 25:44–46)

Bryan was compelled to action by his lament of the injustice he witnessed, and his lament cemented his heart deeper in what breaks God's heart. As a follower of Jesus, Bryan believes that the church has an imperative to get involved in issues of injustice in the world:[14]

For me, faith had to be connected to works—you have to do something with what you believe in some way that reflects and expresses your belief.

> Faith is connected to struggle; that is, while we
> are in this condition we are called to build the
> kingdom of God.[15]

He is the founder and executive director of the Equal Justice Initiative (EJI). Located in Montgomery, Alabama, EJI is a human rights organization. As a result of his passion, the EJI has "won major legal challenges eliminating excessive and unfair sentencing, exonerating innocent death row prisoners, confronting abuse of the incarcerated and the mentally ill, and aiding children prosecuted as adults."[16] The tireless efforts of Bryan and his staff have won the reversals, relief, or release from prison for more than 135 erroneously condemned prisoners on death row.[17] They have also won relief for hundreds of others wrongly convicted or unfairly sentenced.[18] This is simply beautiful. Out of a heart of lament, God will cement our hearts in his kingdom and his love of justice:

> He loves righteousness and justice; the earth is full
> of the LORD's unfailing love. (Ps. 33:5)

> For the LORD is righteous; he loves righteous
> deeds. The upright will see his face. (Ps. 11:7)

Pain Sends Us into Our Purpose

At the center of each story—Abigail, Dwayne, Bryan—were mourning over sin, evil, injustice, suffering, and tragedy. Abigail lamented that chronic pain was a thief, robbing her of the life she dreamed of. Dwayne lamented how his sin stole his marriage. Bryan lamented the miscarriage of justice that he witnessed toward inmates on death row and the poor.

Abigail, Dwayne, and Bryan all lamented, and all three have allowed God to use their pain to bring them solace and to bring others comfort through their stories.

Lamenting the way things are tied to longing for the way things ought to be. In addition to lamenting the state of the sin-infected world, they longed for a world cured by the gospel, a world completely invaded by the kingdom of God in Christ. Before we can be on mission, living in and for God's kingdom, were must lament the idolatry and injustice of the world. This pain, seen in the light of the cross, sends us into our purpose. Out of a broken heart, we cry out to God, and his comforting grace moves us to be comforters.

> Blessed be the God and Father of our Lord Jesus Christ, the Father of mercies and the God of all comfort. He comforts us in all our affliction, so that we may be able to comfort those who are in any kind of affliction, through the comfort we ourselves receive from God. For just as the sufferings of Christ overflow to us, so also through Christ our comfort overflows. (2 Cor. 1:3–5)

The good life is found lamenting the brokenness of the world, longing for the way things ought to be, and helping God make others' lives better.

God's Comfort

First-century Second Temple Jewish people had much to mourn. The pagan, idol-worshiping Romans dominated and oppressed God's people in the promised land. Injustice was a bad odor that filled the air, a toxin that polluted and negatively affected Jew and Gentile alike. Bryan Stevenson makes a keen observation when he writes:,

> An absence of compassion can corrupt the decency
> of a community, a state, a nation. Fear and anger
> can make us vindictive and abusive, unjust and
> unfair until we all suffer the absence of mercy and
> we condemn ourselves as much as we victimize
> others.[19]

Rome was brutal toward the Jews, and many in the Jewish elite religious class were brutal to Jews of the lower social status. The sinners, the chronically sick, and the tax collectors were considered unclean by the Jewish religious establishment; thus, they were forbidden to participate in Jewish religious life. Jesus comforted the rejected ones and those who mourned. It was unheard of for a rabbi to share a meal with the unclean, but Jesus was a different kind of rabbi. He is the Messiah. He does not have to preserve his cleanness from the unclean; he makes the unclean clean.

I often wish I could have seen with my own eyes the meal that Jesus shared with the infamous sinner Matthew, the tax collector.

> While he was reclining at the table in the house,
> many tax collectors and sinners came to eat with
> Jesus and his disciples. When the Pharisees saw
> this, they asked his disciples, "Why does your
> teacher eat with tax collectors and sinners?"
> Now when he heard this, he said, "It is not
> those who are well who need a doctor, but those

who are sick. Go and learn what this means: I desire mercy and not sacrifice. For I didn't come to call the righteous, but sinners." (Matt. 9:10–13)

Jesus is the doctor who performs surgery with a scalpel called mercy. He does not write healing prescriptions in ink but in his blood. As the Great Physician, he also gives the sick universal health insurance, in which he assumes the debt and pays for all the expenses.

Sadly, many of the Jewish religious leaders were infested with sin-sickness, and their homemade remedies of religiosity only made them more hostile toward Jesus. Many of the Pharisees and Sadducees, two leading Jewish religious groups, were known for their religious sacrifice, but not known for giving mercy to the sinner, the sick, and the outcast. Jesus mourned over Jerusalem and their rejection of him:

"Jerusalem, Jerusalem, who kills the prophets and stones those who are sent to her. How often I wanted to gather your children together, as a hen gathers her chicks under her wings, but you were not willing! See, your house is left to you desolate. For I tell you, you will not see me again until you say, 'Blessed is he who comes in the name of the Lord'!" (Matt. 23:37–39)

Jesus lamented how the Pharisees and Sadducees were hypocrites who "shut the door of the kingdom of heaven in people's faces," preventing their entry (Matt. 23:13). He lamented how the dark power had corrupted those who were to lead the people into God's kingdom, and that they were themselves "whitewashed tombs," a brood of vipers, full of greed and self-indulgence (Matt. 23:15–33). Jesus yearned to gather the Jewish people under his wings, but like the prophets of old, he was rejected and ultimately nailed to a cross.

In the Old Testament, one of the metaphors for God is that he is an eagle hovering above his children and protecting them under his wings. The Great Eagle himself had landed; he was among them, but they shooed him away:

> He watches over his nest like an eagle and hovers
> over his young; he spreads his wings, catches him,
> and carries him on his feathers. (Deut. 32:11)

> How priceless your faithful love is, God! People
> take refuge in the shadow of your wings. (Ps. 36:7)

Jesus lamented the state of things as they were. He was the happiest person ever to live, yet he was still called "a man of sorrows" (Isa. 53:3 NLT). Lament was not absent from Jesus' life. He can relate to us in every way.

Come Messiah, Come Messiah

As you can see, there was much to mourn in the promised land. The Jews were waiting for the Messiah to come and cleanse the land of the Gentiles and save God's people through a new exodus. Jesus knew what the prophet Isaiah said concerning God and comforting those who mourn. Also as Israel's long-awaited Messiah and King, he reframed the prophet Isaiah's words around his life and redemptive activity:

> The Spirit of the Lord God is on me,
> because the Lord has anointed me
> to bring good news to the poor.
> He has sent me to heal the brokenhearted,
> to proclaim liberty to the captives
> and freedom to the prisoners;
> to proclaim the year of the Lord's favor,
> and the day of our God's vengeance;
> to comfort all who mourn,
> to provide for those who mourn in Zion;
> to give them a crown of beauty instead of ashes,
> festive oil instead of mourning,
> and splendid clothes instead of despair.
> And they will be called righteous trees,
> planted by the Lord
> to glorify him. (Isa. 61:1–3)

Many of the Jewish people were hoping and longing for mercy, grace, and justice. They longed for God's kingdom to come and lamented the apparent absence of that kingdom. As I noted in the previous chapter, when Jesus stood in his hometown synagogue and read and applied the words of the prophet Isaiah to himself (Luke 4:16–19), he was announcing the arrival of God's kingdom, the new exodus, and his victory over the dark powers that enslaved, blinded, and oppressed humanity.

As Jesus read Isaiah 61:1–3 and affirmed that he was the one who would fulfill this prophecy, in a sudden turn of events, Jesus announced that the Messiah would even bring the brutal Romans into his kingdom (Luke 4:24–30). Often, we miss the reality that those who brutalize and oppress others can be even more injured than the people they harm. Jesus' hometown synagogue liked what he was saying until he said that the Messiah was inviting their non-Jewish enemies into God's kingdom. They wanted the Messiah to make Israel great again, but Jesus came to announce that the doors of God's kingdom have flung wide open to the sick, the sinner, the tax collector—yes to the Pharisee and the Sadducee, but also even the religiously mixed, biracial Samaritans,

> **JESUS CAME TO BUILD A MULTICOLORED KINGDOM JUST LIKE GOD HAD PROMISED ABRAHAM HE WOULD.**

and the pagan, Jew-oppressing, death-dealing Romans. Jesus came to build a multicolored kingdom just like God had promised Abraham he would (Gen. 12:1–3; Gal. 3:8).[20] God's kingdom was open to all sorts of sinners, Jews and the rest of the nations of the world (*ethnos*).

This is the good life: having so much love in your heart that you even invite enemies to sit at your table and eat, to taste the benefits of your kingdom.

We, Not Just Me

As Western Christians, we are okay at mourning our personal sin. Please hear me—mourning our personal sin is not wallowing in self-pity and self-absorption. Wallowing in self-pity and self-absorption is sin itself because it's laced with pride. It is unhelpful shame. When we are bowed down with this kind of self-focus, we are thinking more about our failure than Jesus' accomplishments on our behalf.

On the other hand, to lament over our personal sin is to be broken by godly sorrow. It leads to repentance and praise. We praise God because the blood of Jesus wipes away our sin. It's nailed to the cross and left there forever.

Because Jesus is our representative and we are eternally united to him by faith through the Holy Spirit, his accomplishments and obedience are transferred to us. Our names are forever written in God's will, so we inherit all that Jesus inherits.

Jesus is the one who makes the unrighteous righteous.

Jesus is the one who makes the unclean clean.

Jesus is the one who forgives all our sins—past, present, and future.

Our favored status in the Messiah is unalterable, unchanging, forever grounded in his victory on our behalf. We eternally belong to the King. Therefore, when we lament our sin, it leads to repentance and praise: "Blessed be the Lord! Day after day he bears our burdens; God is our salvation" (Ps. 68:19).

We are terrible, however, at mourning the corporate sins of the church. Our Western way of looking at the world is very individualistic; the Bible corrects our individualism. It not only deals with the individual, but with the corporate. The moment we are born again, we are born into a community—the church. We have a corporate identity, not just an individual identity. For example, the prophet Isaiah said, "Woe is me for I am ruined because I am a man of unclean lips and live among a people of unclean lips" (Isa. 6:5). He identifies himself and the people of Israel as having sinned against God. Personal and corporate lament. It was not enough to lament his personal sin; as a member of God's covenant community, how he and others in the community lived mattered to God. Israel was to be a missionary community to reach the Gentiles and display the goodness of God:

> "I will also make you a light for the nations, to be
> my salvation to the ends of the earth." (Isa. 49:6)

Why would the nations want to follow Israel's God if God's people were no different than the nations?

As members of God's new covenant community called the church, how we live corporately matters. Therefore, when the church sins, we need to lament and repent, not just individually, but together.

Just think of the Lord's Prayer: "Forgive us our sins" (Matt. 6:12 NLT). Notice the "us" and the "our." Following Jesus is more than just me; it's about "we," for God's glory.

Followers of Jesus are called "the body of Christ" (1 Cor. 12:27). Back in the day, grandmas and grandpas would tell their children before they left the house, "Remember your last name and the family you represent." This meant that the actions of the children reflected the entire family. This type of culture led to accountability and responsibility. Likewise, we are members of the body of Christ; the way we live reflects on all of us. That's why the apostle Paul said to live "worthy of the gospel of Christ" (Phil. 1:27). People are watching, and the sin of the one reflects on the whole.

As followers of Jesus, it's vital to our discipleship that we learn to lament the scandals, the abuse, the racism, the misogyny, and other egregious sins in the church. When we understand the corporate identity of Christ's body, we no longer have the option of washing our hands of the sins of other Christians. Lament is entering into what breaks God's heart and knowing God is near the brokenhearted. Lament moves us to action. What does this action look like?

First, we ask God the Holy Spirit to search our own hearts so we may repent of our personal sins. Second, we ask Jesus to start a revival in our own individual life. I often ask God, *Please do in me what I want to see in your church; make me holy, for you are holy.* Third, we corporately confess our sins and ask forgiveness from the people we have hurt. Fourth, we make restitution to those we have wronged. We try to right our wrongs. Fifth, we seek to hold pastors and leaders in the church responsible and accountable to hurtful actions. Sixth, church leadership must teach and equip the congregation through the area where a wrong was committed. For example, if a church has been cruel and unkind to people in the LGBTQ community, the church should equip its congregation to be loving, kind, and gracious, even though they disagree with the LGBTQ community's perspective on sexual ethics. Agreeing with someone is not a prerequisite in order to love someone. Besides, it's the kindness of the Lord that brings people to repentance (Rom. 2:4).

Lament moves us to action.

Happy are those who lament, for they will be cemented in God's comfort.

--- Marinate on This ---

Prayer

Blessed Trinity,

you are not distant or disinterested in us.

Thank you that I can approach your throne of
grace and mercy in my time of need.

In every moment of every season, including
moments of disappointment, doubt, and despair,
you have determined to be present with us.

You enter our worst moments and teach us how
to lament and long for a day when all wrongs are
made right, when tears of sorrow turn to tears of
joy, when hurts are healed.

Teach me to lament well.

Teach me to cry out to you.

May my lament over our broken world be a
battle cry of victory, for in Christ, we are more
than conquerors in him who loved us.

As I lament, encourage my heart and cement
me eternally in the truth that nothing will ever
separate me from the love of God in Christ Jesus.

In Jesus' name, amen.

Questions for Reflection

1. What has been your experience with lamenting? Have you been around someone who is experiencing deep lament? Did it make you uncomfortable?

2. Read Psalm 34:18. Does this verse bring you any comfort? How have you felt God's presence in the midst of pain?

3. This chapter included three stories of lament. Is there one particular story you connect with? At the center of each story is mourning over sin, evil, injustice, suffering, and tragedy. How have you mourned these things in your own life or the lives of others?

4. Pain sends us into our purpose. Have you been able to find purpose in your pain? If you haven't yet, take some time to pray and ask God to reveal the purpose.

5. Western society is individualistic, but the Bible corrects that imbalance by reminding us of our corporate identity. How can we move from an individualistic view of faith to a corporate view of faith?

Things to Remember

1. Those who lament will be cemented in God's comfort.

2. God's greatest goal, his unrelenting aim and passion, is to form Christ in us.

3. Suffering produces endurance. Endurance leads to proven character. Proven character produces hope because the love of God is poured into our hearts.

4. God lovingly enters our suffering and is broken on a cross to heal our brokenness.

5. Pain sends us into our purpose. Out of a broken heart, we cry out to God, and his comforting grace moves us to be comforters.

6. Jesus' accomplishments and obedience are transferred to us.

7. *Lament* means entering into what breaks God's heart and knowing God is near the brokenhearted. Lament moves us to action.

CHAPTER 4

Happy Are the Humble

*"Blessed are the humble, for they will
inherit the earth." (Matthew 5:5)*

W e often think humility is timidity, shyness, or even weakness. But we are wrong. The humility that God imparts to us takes root in the soil of our souls, and as we water and fertilize it by faith, courage and conviction begin to grow in us. We become stronger because our confidence is in God, not ourselves. Instead of having self-confidence, we have *Godfidence.*

Think about it: Jesus was not timid, shy, or weak, yet he was the humblest man ever to live. By grace, he wants to teach us how to live as humble citizens of his kingdom.

God's grace has a humbling power that will redirect your life. Humility is not weakness. Humility is placing yourself under the grace, glory, love, and mission of God. It gives you a supernatural ability to accomplish God's mission. Happy are the humble, for God will do above and beyond all they think or imagine, because the risen Lord Jesus will work mightily in them.

When the sum of who we are is found in all of who Christ is, we become courageous. When we locate our hopes in what Jesus hopes for, we grow in conviction. When we give Jesus the broken pieces of our lives, we grow in completeness.

Jesus' courage, convictions, and completeness (holiness) become ours.

In loving Jesus, we begin to love ourselves. This love for God and self catapults us to love others. This is the good life.

One Man, Two Lives

There were two men—one who had courage, conviction, and completeness, the other who didn't. One man was asked, "Do you know Jesus of Nazareth?" Not only did this man deny that he followed Jesus, despite being with him daily for three years, but he denied that he knew him three times, even cursing and swearing.

The other man followed Jesus with such love and allegiance that the Sanhedrin, the chief Jewish council who exercised authority in civil and religious matters, observed his boldness, wisdom, and power and recognized that he was a follower of Jesus (Acts 4:13). Even under threats, this man would not deny Jesus. He said, "Whether it's right in the sight of God for us to listen to you rather than to God, you decide; for we are unable to stop speaking about what we have seen and heard" (Acts 4:19–20).

One man denied knowing Jesus. Another man was unable to deny Jesus.

Ready for the plot twist? These two men were actually the same person.

Before the resurrection of Jesus, the apostle Peter denied being Jesus' disciple. After the resurrection, he became the leader of Jesus' followers. What happened to Peter to bring about this change? *Jesus* happened to him. He encountered the humbling grace of God, a grace that will remake you and take you deeper into God's kingdom. God's grace will turn a denier of the faith into a defender of the faith, a coward into a courageous leader.

Over the years of journeying with Jesus, I have grown to love Peter. Peter gives me hope. At moments he is loyal, dependable, and wise. At other moments, he's running from servant girls who question him about knowing Jesus. Sometimes he's rebuking Jesus and other times Jesus is rebuking him. Peter at times is brave enough to walk on water, and at others his bravery is severely lacking. There's a little of Peter in all of us.

Fishing Is Sacred

My best childhood memories are fishing with my grandmother. My grandmother and I had a special bond. I called her just about every day from the day I left for college to the day she died. Once I was asked by a Christian counselor to draw a picture of my happiest moments as a child. I drew a picture of my grandmother and me fishing. To this day, I love fishing. Even if I don't catch any fish, it's still a good day because it brings back so many precious memories.

On Fridays, I often go fishing for my Sabbath or rest day. My fishing guide and I are extreme opposites. He's 6'5" with a massive beard and long, wild-looking hair; I'm smaller, clean-shaven, with a shorter hairstyle. He is a South Carolina country boy, and I am a city dude from San Antonio, Texas. He's always coming up with phrases I've never heard, like, "Me and momma gonna have a whee-hooper." Translation: "My wife and I are expecting a baby." Maybe it's our extreme differences that make us good fishing buddies and friends.

The first time I went fishing with him, we caught so many big blue catfish, my shoulders, back, and biceps were sore for three days. But it's not all about the fishing. He and I have had some intense, healing, trust-building conversations on the lake. We talk about everything from politics and racism to marriage, parenting, and football. Some beautiful things happen on the lake while we're fishing.

The apostle Peter also had some beautiful things happen on the lake while fishing. One day Peter was on Lake Gennesaret, which is called the Sea of Galilee. Jesus was also at the lake that day, teaching. The crowds were growing and pressing into him, so he got an empty boat that belonged to Peter. He asked Peter to move the boat away from the shore so he could teach the people. The crowds then sat down to listen. After Jesus finished teaching, he told Peter to move the boat to deep water and drop his net. Peter responded, "We've worked hard all night long and caught nothing. But if you say so, I'll let down the nets" (Luke 5:5). Look what happened next:

> When they did this, they caught a great number
> of fish, and their nets began to tear. So they sig-
> naled to their partners in the other boat to come
> and help them; they came and filled both boats so
> full that they began to sink. (Luke 5:6–7)

Peter encountered Christ, and his life began to change. He was humbled in several ways. First, Peter was humbled by the *sovereignty* of God. Jesus, the Messiah, even commands the fish. If you look back at Peter's initial response to Jesus, you'll catch a hint of sarcasm. "We [the professional fishers, thank you very much] have worked hard all night and caught nothing. But if *you* say so . . ." Peter wasn't humble. He was prideful. He thought he knew more about the fish than Jesus did. But Jesus revealed his sovereignty even over the fish, and Peter caught so many that he needed his partners to help.

Second, Peter was humbled by the *holiness* of God. I suspect the combination of Jesus' teaching and this fishing experience opened Peter's eyes to his sin and Jesus' holiness. Peter literally fell at Jesus' feet with a bunch of slimy fish flopping around him. The more clearly we see God's holiness, the more clearly we see our sin; the more we appreciate God's grace, the more we desire to obey Jesus.

Third, Peter was humbled by a *gracious call*. Jesus tells Peter not to be afraid, and that from now on, he will catch people in the net of the kingdom of God. God's grace always calls us to ministry and mission. God never gives us grace just to give us grace; grace forms a partnership between Jesus and his kingdom business. It was Peter who said every follower of Jesus is a "royal priest" (1 Pet. 2:9 NLT). We mediate on behalf of our king. What an honor! We become missionaries of grace, ambassadors of hope, and agents of reconciliation through our everyday vocations (job, school, family, friendships, etc.).

> **GRACE FORMS A PARTNERSHIP BETWEEN JESUS AND HIS KINGDOM BUSINESS.**

Marinate on how Luke records Peter's encounter with Jesus:

> When Simon Peter saw this, he fell at Jesus's knees and said, "Go away from me, because I'm a sinful

man, Lord!" For he and all those with him were amazed at the catch of fish they had taken, and so were James and John, Zebedee's sons, who were Simon's partners.

"Don't be afraid," Jesus told Simon. "From now on you will be catching people." Then they brought the boats to land, left everything, and followed him. (Luke 5:8–11)

Who Do You Say I Am?

Jesus took his disciples to Caesarea Philippi, where he asked them, "Who do people say that the Son of Man is?" (Matt. 16:13). The term "Son of Man" is a title for Israel's Messiah (Dan. 7:13). Everything Jesus does is intentional. He is about to proclaim his kingdom and how it will never be overcome by the dark powers right in the heart of the kingdom of darkness in Caesarea Philippi.

In the Old Testament, Caesarea Philippi was called Bashan; this area was thought to be the gateway to the Underworld, the realm where the powers of darkness exist. In the New Testament, Caesarea Philippi became the center for the worship of Pan, a Greek god of wilderness and nature. There was also a temple dedicated to Zeus, the ultimate god in the Greco-Roman pantheon.[1] At the back of these pagan temples were caves that led down into the mountain, symbolizing passage into the Underworld, the realm of the dark powers. It was quite audacious that Jesus would take his ragamuffin group of disciples into the heart of an area known for pagan worship. It's as if Jesus, surrounded by these massive temples with cultic worship going on, sets the stage for his disciples: no matter how daunting the kingdom of darkness looks, it will not overcome my kingdom of light.

The same is true today. The kingdom of darkness may howl and rage against you, but the kingdom of God in you will not be overcome.

> Now we have this treasure in clay jars, so that this extraordinary power may be from God and not from us. We are afflicted in every way but not crushed; we are perplexed but not in despair; we are persecuted but not abandoned; we are struck down but not destroyed. We always carry the death of Jesus in our body, so that the life of Jesus may also be displayed in our body. (2 Cor. 4:7–10)

This is what happiness looks like. Happiness is not the absence of bad circumstances; it is the presence of *Godfidence*—certainty and hope in God despite the circumstances. The happy know that the extraordinary power of God is flowing in and through them. Despite being crushed, persecuted, and struck down, a *Godfident* person will not be destroyed because the life of Jesus will be on display in and through them. This is the good life.

In answer to his question about who people said he was, some of Jesus' disciples said that people thought he was Elijah, John the Baptist, or Jeremiah. But then Jesus asked them, "Who do you say that I am?" (Matt. 16:15). Peter boldly said, "You are the Messiah, the Son of the living God" (Matt. 16:16).

> Jesus responded, "Blessed are you, Simon son of Jonah, because flesh and blood did not reveal this

to you, but my Father in heaven. And I also say to you that you are Peter, and on this rock I will build my church, and the gates of Hades will not overpower it. I will give you the keys of the kingdom of heaven, and whatever you bind on earth will have been bound in heaven, and whatever you loose on earth will have been loosed in heaven." Then he gave the disciples orders to tell no one that he was the Messiah. (Matt. 16:17–20)

God *reveals* himself to the humble. Jesus tells Peter, "Blessed [happy] are you, Simon" (Peter's other name). No one has any room to brag about their knowledge of God. The only reason we can see Jesus is because his Father graciously reveals him to us.

God also changes the *name and identity* of the humble. Jesus tells Simon that his name will now be Peter, "the Rock." In the Greek, *petros* means a boulder. Hear the similarity? A boulder is hard to move. Jesus knew that Peter would deny him, yet he named him the Rock because he knew one day Peter would live up to his name and would be a boulder of the faith. God gives us a new name that forms our identity and shapes our future. Simon the uneducated fisherman becomes Peter, a pillar and leader in the early church.

From Denier to Defender

Unfortunately, before Simon could truly become Peter, he had to be shaped by difficult circumstances. As Jesus was preparing for the cross, he told his disciples that they would abandon him. Peter boldly responded that even if everyone else abandoned him, Peter *never* would (Matt. 26:33, 35). Jesus told Peter that, in fact, he would deny Jesus not just once, but three times that night (Matt. 26:34). As Jesus was being led like a lamb to slaughter, Matthew records Peter's actions:

> Then he started to curse and to swear with an oath, "I don't know the man!" Immediately a rooster crowed, and Peter remembered the words Jesus had spoken, "Before the rooster crows, you will deny me three times." And he went outside and wept bitterly. (Matt. 26:74–75)

Peter cried at the memory of what Jesus had told him. I suspect in that moment Peter was confronted with the reality of his weakness. We all share that weakness. We are prone to blowing it big when we place our confidence in our strength instead of God's. I have found over the years that I am stronger by realizing that any moment I can sin and shipwreck my life, family, and church. Therefore, God the Holy Spirit prompts us to keep a posture of humility and neediness of God's sin-defeating grace. Peter thought too highly of himself and, then, in the crucible of life, he denied Jesus. But look at what he was able to write after being changed by the Holy Spirit:

> Humble yourselves, therefore, under the mighty hand of God, so that he may exalt you at the proper time, casting all your cares on him, because he cares about you. Be sober-minded, be alert. Your adversary the devil is prowling around like a roaring lion, looking for anyone he can

devour. Resist him, firm in the faith, knowing that the same kind of sufferings are being experienced by your fellow believers throughout the world. (1 Pet. 5:6–9)

Humility allows us to access Jesus' supernatural ability to defeat sin and adversity. The good life is a humble life of leaning on Jesus.

Peter's denial of Jesus weighed heavily on his heart. He watched in horror as Jesus was executed like a common criminal. So, what do you do when you are sad? You do something you love. Peter went back to fishing with the other disciples.

A few days after Jesus had died, as they were fishing, they heard a voice that sounded familiar, but it

WE ARE PRONE TO BLOWING IT BIG WHEN WE PLACE OUR CONFIDENCE IN OUR STRENGTH INSTEAD OF GOD'S.

couldn't be the voice of the one they had followed for three years, because he was dead and had been buried for three days. The man on the shore asked, "Friends . . . you don't have any fish, do you?" (John 21:5). They answered, "No."

The man on the shore then instructed them to cast their net to the other side. Peter and the others did as he instructed. Just like the first time Jesus told them to cast the net on the other side of the boat, and just like the first time, they caught so many fish they could not lift the net (John 21:6). It was then that Peter knew. He *knew* the impossible had become possible—Jesus was alive! He jumped into the water and swam to shore. When he got there, Jesus was cooking fish over a fire. As the rest of the disciples arrived,

Jesus told them to bring some of the 153 fish they had caught so he could cook them breakfast also (John 21:10).

Please do not miss this: *just as Jesus asked for the fish that he gave the disciples by telling them where to place their net, Jesus will never ask you to do anything that he hasn't given to you first.* This is grace. This is what the fourth-century African bishop Augustine had in mind when he prayed, "Oh Lord, command what you will, and give what you command." That is a prayer the Lord loves to answer. The obedience that Jesus requires is supplied by the grace that he first gives us.

Jesus had just defeated sin, death, and the dark powers through his shed blood and by rising from the dead, and now he was on the beach cooking fish! Jesus didn't berate Peter or the disciples for deserting him. He knew that they would abandon him, yet he gave them grace. Why?

Because grace is only for those who blow it.

Because grace is only for the weak.

Because a heart that knows it can't asks for help from the One who can.

After breakfast, Jesus asked Peter three times, "Do you love me?" Jesus does this to rewrite Peter's story. Peter denied Jesus three times and, graciously, Jesus gave Peter three times to reaffirm his love for him. Before Jesus' resurrection, it was over a fire that Peter denied Jesus. After the resurrection, it was also over a fire that Peter affirmed that he loved Jesus. There were two different fires and two different results. What happened? Jesus took Peter through the fire, burning off his pride, so he could receive grace from Jesus' nail-pierced hands.

HUMILITY CONNECTS US TO GOD'S SUPERNATURAL ABILITY.

Humility is not something that originates in us. It originates in God as he drenches us with grace. It was grace that made Peter into the boulder of faith. Humility connects us to God's supernatural ability.

Enemies Become Friends

Peter's story did not end that day on the beach. He continued to preach the gospel, heal the sick, cast out demons, and build the church. Eventually, God opened his eyes even further.

In Acts 10, we read about a powerful Roman military leader named Cornelius who had a significant impact on Peter. Cornelius and his Gentile family were what first-century Jews called God-fearers. As a God-fearer, he gave generously to the Jewish synagogue and prayed often to the God of Israel. He was pretty much a Jew, except that he was uncircumcised. An angel came to Cornelius saying:

> "Your prayers and your acts of charity have ascended as a memorial offering before God. Now send men to Joppa and call for Simon, who is also named Peter. He is lodging with Simon, a tanner, whose house is by the sea." (Acts 10:4–6)

After this encounter with the angel, Cornelius ordered his soldiers to go to Joppa and find Peter. The next day, as Peter was praying on the roof of a house, God gave him a dream telling him to eat what Jewish people considered unclean food. (The food laws were one of the ethnic badges that separated Jews from Gentiles.) In response to the dream, Peter said, "No, Lord! For I have never eaten anything impure and ritually unclean." Then God said, "What God has made clean, do not call impure" (Acts 10:14–15).

While Peter was struggling with the theology lesson, the soldiers sent by Cornelius found him. The next day Peter arrived with them in Caesarea where he met Cornelius and his entire family. Cornelius fell at Peter's feet, but Peter lifted him up, and said, "You know it's forbidden for a Jewish man to associate with or visit a foreigner, but God has shown me that I must not call any person impure or unclean" (Acts 10:28).

Wow! There it is. Peter's ethnocentrism and prejudice are exposed and healed. It takes humility to admit your racism or prejudice. As a Jew, Peter expressed how many Jews felt about Gentiles in the first century. Humility has the power to heal racial divides—if we allow it.

Peter then preached a sermon to a room full of Gentiles:

> "Now I truly understand that God doesn't show favoritism, but in every nation the person who fears him and does what is right is acceptable to him. He sent the message to the Israelites, proclaiming the good news of peace through Jesus Christ—he is Lord of all." (Acts 10:34–36)

Context is so important. For the Jewish people who experienced slavery for four hundred years under the oppression of the Gentile Egyptians; attacks from the Gentile Canaanites, Amorites, Hivites, Jebusites, and Perizzites; captivity from the Gentile Babylonians; and now oppression from the Gentile Romans, making peace with a people who oppressed them was a work of grace. There was a dark history between Jews and Gentiles, but Jesus was using Peter to reconcile these peoples into the new family of God. During the sermon, the Holy Spirit fell on this sacred moment, and Cornelius and his household believed and were baptized (Acts 10:44–48).

Humility provides the supernatural ability to turn a foe into a friend, an enemy into family.

Humility Is Strong Enough to Serve

The disciples had heard Jesus teach, "Blessed are the humble, for they will inherit the earth" (Matt. 5:5). The Greek word *praeia* means "meek or humble" and conveys the idea of power that is under control. It's like a stallion that has learned to heed the commands of its rider. Happy are those whose power is found in God, not themselves.

To "inherit the earth" simply means to gain citizenship and vice-regency (authority under God) in the new heavens and new earth. The new creation will be populated by the humble—those who lean on the work of Jesus' life and not their abilities. After the resurrection of humanity, everyone in the new heavens and new earth will only brag about Jesus. People who have been humbled by grace always point to the giver of grace. Eternity will have one boast: "Worthy is the Lamb of God."

While Jesus was with his disciples, before he went to the cross, he had another lesson for them on humility. It was the time of Passover, when Jews celebrated their freedom from Egypt. Jesus had walked with and trained his students for three years, but now it was time for him to die for the sins of the world. He was giving his final instructions to his disciples. It would be these men who would lead

God's people to embody God's kingdom on earth. It was in this crucial hour that Jesus had another lesson to teach to his disciples.

Jesus had taught about humility and lived a life of humility, yet pride, like a fork-tongued serpent, rose among the disciples. Listen to Luke describe this scene: "Then a dispute also arose among them about who should be considered the greatest" (Luke 22:24). How about that: the disciples had the best teacher of all—Jesus. His theology was perfect, and he perfectly lived out his theology. Yet, the disciples began to argue about who would be the greatest in God's kingdom.

Pride will destroy a person, a family, a church. It erodes everything. Pride desires attention and credit. It is competitive and doesn't like to share or to see anyone else do well. Jesus, being full of mercy, teaches his disciples once again: you are not to lead like the Gentiles, lording and bullying people. We are not tyrants; we are servants (Mark 10:42–44). He then does the unthinkable: Jesus washes the feet of the disciples.

First, Jesus was humble enough to perform the task of a slave. The humility of God is overwhelming. How could God the Son wash the feet of disciples who were arguing about who would be the greatest? Once again, Jesus doesn't run out of grace and patience with his disciples.

It's in experiencing his grace and patience that we become humble enough to serve others. Eventually, each disciple went on to serve others with such love that they all gave their lives for the sake of God's kingdom. The only one who was not killed was John, and he ended up being exiled on the island of Patmos. If Jesus was humble enough to serve, we should seek to serve and not to be served.

Second, in God's economy, great people are humble enough to become great servants. Instead of living for others to serve you, you live to serve others as an act of worship. We move from being self-centered to others-centered because our lives are centered on Jesus.

Happy people are selfless, servant-hearted people. Unhappy people are entitled. Dr. Martin Luther King Jr. once said:

> Everybody can be great, because everybody can serve. You don't have to have a college degree to serve. You don't have to make your subject and your verb agree to serve. You don't have to know about Plato and Aristotle to serve. You don't have to know Einstein's theory of relativity to serve. You don't have to know the second theory of thermodynamics in physics to serve. You only need a heart full of grace, a soul generated by love.[2]

I have found in my own life that if I give more than I take, I'm happier. When I think about Jesus carrying my cross and my sin and that he loved me and served me, how could I not want to serve others?

> Jesus called them over and said to them, "You know that those who are regarded as rulers of the Gentiles lord it over them, and those in high positions act as tyrants over them. But it is not so among you. On the contrary, whoever wants to become great among you will be your servant, and whoever wants to be first among you will be a slave to all. For even the Son of Man did not come

to be served, but to serve, and to give his life as a
ransom for many." (Mark 10:42–45)

Third, by washing the filthy feet of his disciples, Jesus symbolized how he would die for our filthy sins as a fulfillment of the "Suffering Servant" prophecy in Isaiah 53:

> We all went astray like sheep; we all have turned
> to our own way; and the LORD has punished him
> for the iniquity of us all. (v. 6)

Fourth, in first-century Greco-Roman society, the Romans did not value humility. Judaism, for the most part, did value humility. In the Greco-Roman world, humility was weakness. In the Jewish world, it was a virtue. In washing his disciples' feet, Jesus overturned positions of social status: the King performed the task of a servant. He was embodying the beauty of humility. The greatest among you should be the greatest servants—that's the way of the kingdom.

Meditate on this hymn that the early church sang about Jesus:

> Adopt the same attitude as that of Christ Jesus,
> who, existing in the form of God,
> did not consider equality with God
> as something to be exploited.
> Instead he emptied himself
> by assuming the form of a servant,
> taking on the likeness of humanity.
> And when he had come as a man,
> he humbled himself by becoming obedient
> to the point of death—
> even to death on a cross.

> For this reason God highly exalted him
> and gave him the name
> that is above every name,
> so that at the name of Jesus
> every knee will bow—
> in heaven and on earth
> and under the earth—
> and every tongue will confess
> that Jesus Christ is Lord,
> to the glory of God the Father. (Phil. 2:5–11)

Happy are the humble, for they are the ones becoming like Jesus.

——————————— Marinate on This ———————————

Prayer

Spirit of the living God,

May my soul find confidence in Jesus alone.

He is the strength I do not possess.

He is the grace that I lack.

He is all that I long for and was created for.

Lord Jesus,

May I boast in my weaknesses so the Father's
strength would be my strength.

Help me to find comfort in his faithful love.

Help me find my identity in his unending love.

Help me never forget that his grace is sufficient.

Father,

May my inability give way to the supernatural
ability of the Holy Spirit.

Help me to walk in humility, patience, kindness,
and mercy.

Help me to see how great Jesus is so I can be
continually in awe and humbled by him.

"God opposes the proud but gives grace to the humble" (James 4:6 NLT).

In Jesus' name, amen

Questions for Reflection

1. Peter went from being a denier of the faith to a defender of the faith. How can you relate to Peter? Have you experienced moments of weakness in your faith?

2. How did your life begin to change when you first encountered Christ? How have you been humbled by God's sovereignty and holiness?

3. God's grace always calls us to ministry and mission. From grace comes purpose, and that purpose is to be an agent of grace in our communities. What specific ways can you minister and live on mission in your everyday life?

4. What is the difference between confidence and *Godfidence*? How can you move from confidence to *Godfidence* in your life?

5. Dr. Martin Luther King Jr. talked about how everyone— regardless of status or so-called qualification—can serve. Can you recall someone in your life who may not have been great in the eyes of the world, but was a great and humble servant?

6. After reading the chapter, how has your view of humility changed? Do you view humility as a strength? How can you begin to cultivate true humility in your life?

Things to Remember

1. Humility is placing yourself under the grace, glory, and mission of God.

2. Humility gives us supernatural ability to accomplish God's mission.

3. The more we see God's holiness, the more we see our sin; the more we appreciate God's grace, the more we desire to obey Jesus.

4. Grace forms a partnership between Jesus and us to be about his kingdom business.

5. The kingdom of darkness may howl and rage against you, but the kingdom of God in you will not be overcome.

6. The obedience that Jesus requires is supplied by the grace he first gives us.

CHAPTER 5

Happy Are the Hungry and Thirsty

"Blessed are those who hunger and thirst for righ-
teousness, for they will be filled." (Matthew 5:6)

I long for sad things to be untrue one day. I hunger for wrongs to
be made right. I thirst for the hurt to be healed and the broken
to be fixed. I want decay and death to give way to life and human
flourishing.

Like you, I'm longing for God's justice and *shalom* (peace) to
overwhelm our unjust world.

And as I long for the brokenness out there to be healed, I also
desire the brokenness in me to be healed.

As I sit down at my desk at Transformation Church to write,
my heart aches. Like the rest of America, I'm reeling from another
mass shooting. Domestic terrorism and gun violence are running
rampant. There have been more mass shootings than days this year.[1]
My heart breaks as I read another story about child sexual abuse
being covered up by religious leaders who were supposed to represent Christ and protect children. My heart aches at the thought of
the homeless, many of whom are mentally ill, who will sleep on the
street tonight.[2] My heart also hurts at the thought of the thousands

of abortions that will happen today and the many other injustices that occur daily in our broken, grieving world.

Perhaps some of you reading these words will say, "There *can't* be a god with all this injustice, suffering, and ugliness, and if there is, he can't be powerful and loving." I get it. I understand. Please, just keep reading. Because whether or not you realize it now, your anger, disappointment, and desire for the ugly realities of our broken world to be fixed are a longing for the beauty of God.

How do we know something is unjust unless we believe there is a standard of justice?

Why do we get angry and hurt by suffering unless we know it shouldn't be that way?

How do we know a line is crooked unless there is a straight line to compare it to?

If we long for goodness, beauty, and justice, there must be One who created these things. That Creator must exhibit those things because you can't give away what you do not possess. As we yell and shake our fists at all the wrongs in the world, we are longing for God to make the sad things untrue, to make the ugly beautiful, to heal the hurt. We are joining in the song of the ancient Jewish people when they sang, "He loves righteousness and justice; the earth is full of the LORD's unfailing love" (Ps. 33:5). We join the Jewish prophet Amos when he wrote, "But let justice flow like water, and righteousness, like an unfailing stream" (Amos 5:24).

The One True God, that is the Father, the Son, and the Holy Spirit, made creation good, and we messed it up. We introduced death and decay. But God didn't leave us in our mess. Amazingly, he joined us in our brokenness. He even allowed all the sad things that have happened to us to happen to him on the cross. He does this so his resurrection can birth a new creation right in the heart of the old. The righteousness and justice we long for walked out of a tomb in Jerusalem. In Jesus of Nazareth, the triune God became an actor in his own play, and through the power of the Holy Spirit, he wants us to become actors in the divine drama of redemption. We become his agents of redemption.

I want to introduce you to some people who have allowed the Son of God, by God the Holy Spirit's power, to act out his life through their lives for his glory. They have seen the injustice and pain in this world and have hungered and thirsted for righteousness to make a difference. They're living the good life.

Basketball, Shoes, and Snow

One day in Lagos, Nigeria, nine-year-old Manny Ohonme noticed something strange: a white man with a large orange ball. The man was throwing the ball at a basket that was in the air, instead of kicking it into a goal. As Manny observed this odd spectacle, the man asked him if he wanted to enter a contest. The winner would get a pair of shoes. Like most boys in Lagos, owning a pair of shoes was a luxury that his parents could not afford. Sometimes, it's hard for me to walk in my closet because of all my shoes. Manny grew up walking around shoeless, exposing himself to disease. He grew up in a two bedroom cinder-block home with thirteen family members. Most people in his community existed on less than a $1 a day. Manny knew hunger, often only eating one meal a day.

Manny jumped at the chance to win a pair of shoes, even though he had no clue what to do with the orange ball. Somehow, he won the basketball contest, and he got his first pair of shoes. This

"Good Samaritan" was a missionary from Wisconsin, spurred on by the hope-giving, righting-the-wrongs love of Jesus. He transformed Manny's life by his simple act. Manny eventually grew to be 6'4" and became a phenomenal high school basketball player. Colleges in America began to recruit him. But there was one school that captured his eye. This school mailed him a brochure with college students driving a convertible sports car, the sun dancing on their faces, the wind blowing through their hair. They looked so happy. He made his choice.

Manny packed all his belongings, which admittedly weren't much. He hugged his family goodbye and boarded his airplane with a T-shirt, shorts, and sandals. He was on his way to paradise.

Manny arrived in Fargo, North Dakota. In the winter. Instead of sunshine, he discovered that paradise had this cold white stuff all over the ground. Surely he had landed in the wrong place, he thought. Manny had accepted a basketball scholarship to play for a North Dakota college! His first weeks of school, he didn't leave his dorm. He would turn the heater to ninety degrees and just lie in his bed.

Eventually, Manny had a successful basketball career, graduated, met a beautiful woman, and got married. With his work ethic, intelligence, and faith, Manny quickly rose up the corporate ladder. The poor, shoeless boy from Nigeria was living the American Dream.

But something wasn't right in his soul. The thoughts of children being shoeless made him do something that most of his peers thought was crazy. He quit his lucrative job that had given him power, privilege, and prestige to start a nonprofit organization called Samaritan's Feet. Manny and his wife, Tracie, have an audacious goal to give ten million pairs of shoes to children around the world.

Healing can only happen if we are willing to act. The good life is a life that answers God's call to make a positive difference in the world, to be a giver, not a taker. How different will the world be because you existed? You don't have to be famous to make a difference—you just need to be faithful. God doesn't need your ability; he just wants your availability.

Manny and Tracie are actors in God's story of redemptive justice. They are mobilizing thousands of volunteers so millions can be touched by the love of Christ. Sadly, one-third of the world lives on less than two dollars a day. These image-bearers of God can't afford food, housing, or clothing.[3] I've never known what it's like not to have shoes, but 1.5 billion people do know what it's like. As a result of not having shoes, these people are infected with parasitic diseases, which are transmitted through contaminated soil.[4] Manny and Tracie want to give the poorest of the poor shoes so disease can be prevented and so these precious people can know that God has not forgotten them.

Think about this—you are the answer to someone's prayers. Someone is praying right now, and God wants to use you to answer their prayer. The justice the world longs for is found in you. The King of heaven gives you his righteousness so you can express it to the world around you. If Jesus can lay down his life for us, who are we to keep our lives? Paradoxically, when we lay down our lives in service to others, we find the true good life. Happiness is making another image-bearer's life better. Jesus says:

> "If anyone wants to follow after me, let him deny
> himself, take up his cross daily, and follow me.
> For whoever wants to save his life will lose it, but

whoever loses his life because of me will save it."
(Luke 9:23–24)

Happiness is found in meeting another's need.

Happiness is found in healing a hurt.

Happiness is found in becoming God's paintbrush to create beauty where there is ugliness, hope where there is despair, and salvation where there is condemnation.

Before people are given a new pair of shoes, they have their feet washed by the Samaritan's Feet team. Why is this important? To wash someone's feet is an act of acknowledging his or her worth. This act of grace dignifies people and lets them know they are valuable and that their lives matter. Washing someone's feet and giving them a pair of shoes as a gift is a symbol of Jesus and his work on the cross. Not only did Jesus literally wash the feet of his disciples; on the cross, he has washed our sins away and given us his eternal-kind-of-life as a gift. Washing feet is the posture of a servant. Jesus was the ultimate suffering servant who washed our sins away under the shower of his blood. Jesus served us so we could be servants.

We often ask God when we witness suffering or injustice, "Where are you?" I think he responds, "Where are you, Church? I left you on earth and deposited my life in you to continue my ministry and mission. You are my hands and feet. You are salt and light, the great city on a hill" (see Matt. 5:13–16).

God is not looking for ability; he has plenty of that. He's longing for availability to share his supernatural ability. Manny, a poor kid from Lagos, Nigeria, is transforming the world because God has shared his ability with him. Manny is hungering and thirsting for God's righteousness and unfailing, extravagant love to fill the earth.

May we be as hungry and thirsty as Manny to see God's justice touch the injustice of our world.

God can use you right where you are. You don't have to start a nonprofit like Manny and Tracie; you can serve at your local church or start something small to meet the deep needs of the world. There are many opportunities for you to be a blessing. You can make a difference right where you are. As Frederick Buechner put it:

> The place God calls you to is the place where your
> deep gladness and the world's deep hunger meet.[5]

The Day I Went to Prison in South Carolina

A few years back, I went to prison in South Carolina. I didn't plan on going to prison. But sometimes things happen, and you get set up. I was totally set up.

Robert and Pat Vinroot, a married couple in their late sixties, had been volunteering at a South Carolina prison for a while. They just wanted to make a positive difference in these men's lives. Pat read my book, *Hero: Unleashing God's Power in a Man's Heart*, and she wanted to share it with the men she was serving. Her next thought was, *Robert, we need to get this Derwin to speak to the men.* She had no clue that I lived near her in Charlotte. In a matter of days through mutual friends, we connected by phone. They kindly asked me if I would preach at the prison, and it didn't take me long to agree. I've always had a heart for men and women behind bars because I've seen how a community can be ravaged by mass incarceration. One of the most effective ways to cut down on the rate of people returning to prison is by transforming them through the power of the gospel. According to one study by Baylor University,

"Faith-motivated mentors helped prisoners to adopt prosocial values through a process of spiritual development that was critical to helping prisoners remain crime-free after leaving prison."[6]

Several members of Transformation Church and I served in the prison. It is an eerie feeling when you hear the prison doors lock behind you. At the service, the men sang worship songs, their voices booming in unison and beauty. Their hands were raised; tears flowed. Gang members, drug dealers, armed robbers, murderers, white men, black men, Asian men, Latino men—all singing songs of praise to God. I felt so much freedom behind bars with these men. It was a mutual blessing. These men blessed us with their passion, hope, and freedom, and we blessed them by being with them and treating them with dignity and honor.

Since that moment, we have seen multiple men get baptized, get released, and be reconciled with their families. Because of Pat and Robert's passion to bring healing to the hurt, Transformation Church now has more than five prison partnerships. Wardens from other places invite us into their prisons because of the positive changes they have heard about. Often, I get credit for starting these innovative and transformative prison ministries, but the reality is that God put a hunger and thirst in Pat and Robert's hearts. Out of their faith, God has done something uncommon and beautiful. One match can start a forest fire, and one couple in their late sixties were set on fire by Jesus and blazed so brightly that now hundreds of people serve in prison partnerships throughout South Carolina. Are you the next spark to cause a blaze of God's glory? Why not you?

As we continued to serve in our first prison partnership, one particular inmate stood out. He was the worship leader of the music team. He carried himself with quiet confidence and wore humility like a warm coat. You could sense the depth of his discipleship and love for Jesus and his concern for fellow inmates by the way he led. As I got to know him, I was surprised to learn that he was in prison for murder. During a drug-induced rage, he killed his friend. As I talked to him, I could hear the anguish, remorse, and repentance in his voice. He was deeply hurt by the pain that he had caused. He told me that he destroyed two families—his and his friend's. I'm not sure how a person can live without knowing the forgiveness of Jesus when they have taken a life. It was his remorse that drove him to the cross of Jesus where forgiveness and second chances are found.

By the time I met him, he had been in prison for more than twenty years. Each time he went up for parole it was denied. We told him that if he was granted parole, he would have a job on staff at Transformation Church. A few years went by and, eventually, he was released. He is now a staff member at Transformation Church where he serves in our prison ministry, music team, and counseling ministry. He is trying to make amends with the family he hurt. He ministers to prison inmates and counsels hurting people. He is hungering and thirsting for God's righteousness.

Often, God will take our deepest sin, forgive us, renovate our hearts, and give us a ministry to serve those who are in the same dark places we were. This is what the good life looks like. It is a life of repentance, forgiveness, mercy, and serving the hurting. God will take unrighteous people and make them righteous through the blood of Christ, so they can express his righteousness.

How much more then, since we have now been
declared righteous by his blood, will we be saved
through him from wrath. (Rom. 5:9)

He made the one who did not know sin to be sin
for us, so that in him we might become the righteousness of God. (2 Cor. 5:21)

Kids, Education, and Jesus

As we hunger and thirst for righteousness, sometimes the need
is right in our own neighborhood. In one of my sermons, I said that
if our community doesn't get better as a result of our presence, we
shouldn't be here. We wanted to serve our community with such
love, generosity, and compassion that if we were to pack up and
leave, the people of our community would protest because we added
so much value and made the place so much better.

Serving our local public schools was the most effective place
to start. A few staff members and I set up an appointment with
local school principals. The school staff was initially skeptical of
us. They wanted to know what we wanted. When I told them we
simply wanted to serve, they were surprised. I asked how we could
help students, teachers, and staff become more effective. From that
first meeting, we have now expanded to seven school partners in
our community.

One way we serve our partner schools is by providing backpack
meals, which feed students in need each weekend. When we found
out that some kids in our community did not eat much over the
weekend and that their free school lunches were their best meals,
God's love and justice demanded that we do something. Hungry,

undernourished children can't succeed in school. Each week, volunteers prepare bags full of breakfast, lunch, and dinner for two days for each child in need. In the 2018–2019 school year, we collected 62,467 items of food, equaling 28,800 meals for students in our school partnerships.

Another way to serve schools is through staff appreciation. A few times a year we provide a meal or treats to show appreciation for all staff, administration, and teachers. School administrators and staff are underpaid and underappreciated. We want them to know that they are valuable and that we believe in them. Often teachers are the glue that keeps a community together. Teachers and coaches have been the most influential people in my life. Before the new school year, we also provide teachers with bins for each classroom filled with school supplies so they won't have to spend their own money. For goodness' sake, teachers are already underpaid. They shouldn't have to buy school supplies too! We help alleviate this burden by harnessing the collective power and resources of our church. Teamwork really does make the dream work. Together, everyone achieves more. If we all take our little lights and shine them together, we become a city on a hill. With so many problems in the world, it will take our collaborative effort to shine into the darkness.

If the people of God truly hungered and thirsted for God's righteousness, imagine all the good we could do. Here are two beautiful outcomes from serving our community with no strings attached: first, the students, parents, teachers, administrators, and people in our community flood to Transformation Church to learn more about why we do what we do. We have seen thousands of people come to faith in Christ and be baptized because they saw us serve our community with love, generosity, and compassion. We don't want our kids to be hungry, and we do not want our community to be hungry. In addition to food that we provide for students, 810 Transformers (members of Transformation Church) assembled 151,050 meals to help feed hungry people in our community through The Hunger Project.

The words of James, the half-brother of Jesus, echo in our hearts:

> If a brother or sister is without clothes and lacks daily food and one of you says to them, "Go in peace, stay warm, and be well fed," but you don't give them what the body needs, what good is it? In the same way faith, if it doesn't have works, is dead by itself. (James 2:15–17)

The term *works* that James uses expresses that faith compels us to love those in need (James 2:8). We want to love our community well because Jesus loved us. These are just a few examples of Christ-followers acting as the hands and feet of God in a few broken places. There is no shortage of opportunity to find a place to bring God's love. Jesus is a holistic Savior. He fed and healed people. It was often when Jesus met a person's physical need that they opened up to him, meeting their need for salvation.

The Early Christians

Somewhere along the way, the church moved from following this command to more of a "save-your-soul-only" theology. We say we are "just passing through," and sadly, we act like it. We miss that God has left us here as his hands and feet.

This limited gospel is problematic on so many levels. It's poor theology at best and evil at worst. God cares about the whole person and for all of humanity right here and now. It's hard for hungry people to hear the gospel over the sound of a grumbling stomach. It's hard for people to hear "Jesus loves you" when they see Jesus' people being unloving. The early church embodied Jesus' practice of caring for the whole person. It was what they were known for. Author Rodney Stark, in *The Rise of Christianity*, writes:

> Christianity revitalized life in the Greco-Roman cities by providing new norms and new kinds of social relationships able to cope with many urgent urban problems. To cities filled with homeless and the impoverished, Christianity offered charity as well as hope. To cities filled with newcomers and strangers, Christianity offered an immediate basis for attachments. To cities filled with orphans and widows, Christianity provided a new and expanded family. To cities torn by violent strife, Christianity offered a new basis for social solidarity. And to cities faced with epidemics, fires, and earthquakes, Christianity offered effective nursing services.[7]

Tertullian (AD 155–220), a North African church leader, wrote: "It is our care of the helpless, our practice of loving kindness that brands us in the eyes of our opponents . . . they say how they love one another!"[8] May those who disagree with our beliefs see our desire to display the love for Christ through the healing of hurts, feeding the hungry, clothing the naked, and sacrificing ourselves in the cause of justice, and may they say, *"Look, how they love people."*

> Let us not get tired of doing good, for we will reap
> at the proper time if we don't give up. Therefore,
> as we have opportunity, let us work for the good of
> all, especially for those who belong to the house-
> hold of faith. (Gal. 6:9–10)

Jesus, Righteousness, and Satisfaction

As Jesus continued to teach, he said, "Blessed are those who hunger and thirst for righteousness, for they will be filled" (Matt. 5:6). Jesus takes a common human feeling and connects it to God's kingdom. In the ancient Jewish world, people knew what true hunger and thirst were like. Food and water were not as abundant then as they are now. In the Jewish context of the first century, to thirst and hunger for righteousness was to love God with all your being and to love your neighbor the way you love yourself. Jesus understood covenantal faithfulness to the Torah as love for God, self, and neighbor (Matt. 22:37–39). To hunger and thirst for righteousness is to long for love and embody that love at school, at work, in relationships, in parenting, in everything.

Just as a person can't live without food or water, we cannot live without God. We were made to be fueled by God's life and love. He is the only food that will nourish us and the only drink that will satisfy our thirst. As the author of Scripture, Jesus has Isaiah 55:1 in mind:

"Come, everyone who is thirsty, come to the
water; and you without silver, come, buy, and
eat! Come, buy wine and milk without silver and
without cost!"

The food and water we need to live and thrive are free of
charge—we simply must come. Our love for God doesn't originate
in us; it's a response to his gift of eating and drinking at his banquet.
He freely feeds us and gives us all we need to be conformed to the
image of Christ.

Happy people are people who hunger and thirst for righteousness. Jesus echoes the words of the psalmist:

God, you are my God; I eagerly seek you.
I thirst for you;
my body faints for you
in a land that is dry, desolate, and without water.
So I gaze on you in the sanctuary
to see your strength and your glory.

My lips will glorify you
because your faithful love is better than life.
So I will bless you as long as I live;
at your name, I will lift up my hands.
You satisfy me as with rich food;
my mouth will praise you with joyful lips.
(Ps. 63:1–5)

Jesus says those who hunger and thirst for righteousness will be
filled. The word *filled* means to be bloated or gorged. Have you ever
eaten so much that you are just stuffed? I must admit, I have done so

on multiple occasions. Jesus is saying the satisfaction we are looking for is found in God himself.

Happy are those who are fattened, gorged, and overflowing with love for God, for themselves, and for their neighbors. Happy are those who partner with God to meet the deep hurts of the world with his deep love. There's plenty of room at God's banquet table—all the food and drink you want. Come, you're invited to the life you were created for.

> How happy are those who uphold justice, who practice righteousness at all times. (Ps. 106:3)

———————————— Marinate on This ————————————

Prayer

Father,

As your Word says,

"How happy are those who uphold justice,
who practice righteousness at all times"
(Ps. 106:3).

Through the indwelling life of Jesus,

And the infinite power of the Holy Spirit,

Give me an unceasing hunger and thirst for
righteousness,

Glory be to your name, amen.

Questions for Reflection

1. Do you ever have trouble reconciling the "bad" of this world with the existence of God? Have you been able to work through that tension? What conclusions have you drawn?

2. God joins us in our brokenness and even sent Jesus to bring justice once and for all by bearing the injustice of the world. Do you find this comforting? How can we join God in his mission to bring redemption to earth?

3. This chapter included several stories of people who saw brokenness in the world and decided to do something about it. Who have you seen do this well? Are you inspired to make a difference in your community?

4. Read Isaiah 55:1. As you reflect on this verse, what comes to mind? Do you trust God to provide all that is needed for life?

5. Happiness is found in partnering with God to meet the deep needs of this world. How is God calling you to partner with him today?

Things to Remember

1. We are God's agents of grace and redemption.

2. The King of heaven gives you his righteousness so you can express it to the world around you.

3. Happiness is found in becoming God's paintbrush to create beauty where there is ugliness, hope where there is despair, and salvation where there is death.

4. God is not looking for your ability; he longs for your availability to share his supernatural ability.

5. Jesus is a holistic Savior.

6. The good life looks like a life of repentance, forgiveness, mercy, and serving the hurting.

7. God will take unrighteous people and make them righteous through the blood of Christ so they can express his righteousness to the earth.

CHAPTER 6

Happy Are the Merciful

"Blessed are the merciful, for they will
be shown mercy." (Matthew 5:7)

I n the kingdom of God, mercy trumps judgment (James 2:13). However, in the kingdom of man, judgment with its accompanying condemnation trumps mercy.

Do you ever feel like we live in a culture that feeds off the failures and flaws of others? Perhaps social media have increased our propensity to act like a school of piranha, ripping and tearing flesh off the helpless prey until there is nothing left. At the heart of our lack of mercy is our inability to receive mercy. We are not merciful because we have not experienced divine mercy. If you do not possess it, you cannot give it away. Jesus, the One who is the endless fountain of

AT THE HEART OF OUR LACK OF MERCY IS OUR INABILITY TO RECEIVE MERCY.

mercy, was sent to earth so humanity could come and drink the life-giving waters of his mercy. A lack of mercy keeps a person caged in the dungeon of unforgiveness, but living a merciful life is the good life.

Jesus' World

Jesus' world was not that much different from ours. The Roman Empire was not merciful either. For the most part, they ruled with intimidation, violence, and brute force. Even Jesus' disciples were susceptible to the Roman way as they showed the night they argued about who would be the greatest in God's kingdom (as we looked at in chapter 4). As Jesus washed his disciples' feet, he embodied the way of his kingdom, which is servanthood, not self-serving. Instead of giving his disciples the sharp rebuke they deserved, he served them. This is mercy. God is merciful.

After spending three years with the One who is mercy, Jesus' disciples deserved to be rebuked, but instead he washed their dirty feet. Considering their unbridled ambition to pursue power, Jesus withheld judgment and acted out the culture of his Father's kingdom, which is mercy. This act of humility, love, and patience is mercy personified. The ultimate act of mercy is Jesus giving his life as a ransom to carry us with his bloody hands into his Father's kingdom. We didn't deserve salvation. We didn't earn salvation. Salvation is a gift given to us by a merciful God of unending grace.

As the new, better, and final Passover Lamb, Jesus shed his blood to free us from our bondage to sin, death, and evil. When we realize that it is mercy that calls our name when we are running away from him, we are moved to stop, turn around, and follow him. When we realize that it is mercy that takes our place on the cross, we desire a place in his kingdom. When we realize that it is mercy that meets us in the dark, we want to follow him into the light. Those who have experienced divine mercy are themselves shaped and fashioned into merciful people.

Many of the Jewish religious leaders had serious issues with mercy as well. Jesus describes the scribes and Pharisees as those who "don't practice what they teach," who "shut the door of the kingdom of heaven in people's faces," who are "hypocrites" that make people "fit for hell," who are "blind guides," and greedy "snakes" that "have neglected the more important matters of the law—justice, mercy, and faithfulness" (Matt. 23:1–36).

The common Jewish people were caught between the merciless, oppressive Roman Empire and the merciless, compromised Jewish religious establishment. Jesus said that Pharisees and scribes would meticulously tithe ten percent of the spices mint, dill, and cumin, but they lacked justice, mercy, and faithfulness (Matt. 23:23). They obeyed the visible, external parts of the law, but disobeyed the internal matters of the heart, which were far more important in the first place. Instead of pursuing love, many pursued power and status. As Pharisees and scribes, they would have known these Scriptures that reflect God's way of treating others:

> Learn to do what is good. Pursue justice. Correct the oppressor. Defend the rights of the fatherless. Plead the widow's cause. (Isa. 1:17)

> This is what the LORD says: Administer justice and righteousness. Rescue the victim of robbery from his oppressor. Don't exploit or brutalize the resident alien, the fatherless, or the widow. (Jer. 22:3)

> Mankind, he has told each of you what is good and what it is the LORD requires of you: to act

justly, to love faithfulness, and to walk humbly
with your God. (Micah 6:8)

Mercy Came to Us

As we have seen, the first-century world of Jesus was not that
much different than our world. So mercy himself came *to show us a
better way to be human.*

As Jesus continues his manifesto on what it means to be happy,
he says, "Blessed are the merciful, for they will be shown mercy"
(Matt. 5:7). Mercy is not something God does. Mercy is who God
is. When he revealed himself to Moses in Exodus 34:6 (NLT), God
said, "Yahweh! The LORD! The God of compassion and mercy!" It
was one of the first characteristics God used to describe himself.
God's mercy is essential to his being, which is eternal, infinite, and
inexhaustible. God can no more run out of mercy than he can run
out of himself. It's God's mercy that sets his face toward us with eyes
of compassion and hands of tenderness. Mercy is God in Christ, by the
Spirit's power, running toward humanity locked in a burning house
of sin and death. In giving us mercy, he breaks down the door and frees us
from that burning house. He gives us himself so we can truly be
ourselves.

> **GOD CAN NO MORE
> RUN OUT OF MERCY
> THAN HE CAN RUN
> OUT OF HIMSELF.**

Mercy is God presenting himself to us in the midst of our mess.
We only know that Jesus is merciful because he pursues us. Left to
our own devices, we would all go the way of the Pharisees or the
Romans. Many of the Pharisees perverted the worship of the one

true God, and the Romans worshiped a pantheon of false gods. Either way, we would fall into a ditch of despair. But Jesus comes to lift us out of this ditch. He doesn't yell down and say, "Here's a ladder—climb up!" No, he jumps into the pit with us, puts us on his back, and carries us out of the ditch.

Jesus fights for us, even when we're fighting against him. God softens our hearts. As Jesus identifies with our hurts, our fears, and our sin, we can "approach the throne of grace with boldness, so that we may receive mercy and find grace to help us in time of need" (Heb. 4:16). Remember when I said God's mercy is eternal, infinite, and inexhaustible? Because God is eternal, his mercy erases our past sins, is a present help in our time of need, and assures that at the future judgment we will hear, "Therefore, there is now no condemnation for those in Christ Jesus" (Rom. 8:1). Jesus shares his mercy with us *so that* we can become merciful.

The Merciful Samaritan

According to Jesus, merciful people love their neighbors. But the kingdom-of-God-kind-of-love that Jesus is talking about is more than sentimentalism. This love is a commitment to worshiping God by loving people. It's a love fueled by being a recipient of mercy yourself. It's not a love that is doing the act of mercy because you expect to get something in return—that would be a business transaction. Mercy gives for the sake of mercy itself. This love looks like the cross of Jesus.

Let me tell you the story of the "Merciful Samaritan." One day Jesus was talking with an expert in the Jewish Law. It was the expert's task to rightly interpret the Old Testament and to teach the oral Jewish traditions, applying God's Word and the people's history to their current situation. The expert wanted to test Jesus, so he asked, "Teacher, what must I do to inherit eternal life?" (Luke 10:25). He wanted to discredit Jesus and show that this backwoods, poor rabbi from the wrong side of the tracks was not a true teacher.

Jesus responded with a question of his own: "What is written in the law? . . . How do you read it?" (v. 26). The expert answered, "Love the Lord your God with all your heart, with all your soul, with all your strength, and with all your mind," and "your neighbor as yourself" (v. 27).

Jesus responded, "You've answered correctly. . . . Do this and you will live" (v. 28). There it is: Upward, Inward, Outward. Love God, love yourself, love your neighbor. That's the good life.

Then, the one who wanted to trap Jesus was ensnared himself. He started looking for a way out: "But wanting to justify himself, he asked Jesus, 'And who is my neighbor?'" (v. 29).

As a Jew of this time, his neighbor would have been another Jewish man. But Jesus corrected this assumption by telling a story about an unlikely neighbor who displayed mercy to an unlikely recipient.

There was a Jewish man traveling from Jerusalem to Jericho. This journey was a seventeen-mile descent of three thousand feet, full of winding twists and turns. Jesus' audience would have known that the journey was fraught with danger because bandits had multiple hiding places to attack unsuspecting travelers. In the first-century world, it was referred to as the "bloody way" because of the violence that frequently occurred on this route."[1] Unsurprisingly, the bandits beat, stripped, and robbed the Jewish man, leaving him for dead.

As the man lay on the side of the road clinging to life, a Jewish priest and a Levite came down from Jerusalem, saw him, and didn't offer help to him. Priests performed sacrifices, took care of the temple, and taught the Scriptures. The Levites were members of the tribe of Levi who were also tasked with various roles in the temple. Reflect on this Scripture:

> "A priest happened to be going down that road.
> When he saw him, he passed by on the other side.
> In the same way, a Levite, when he arrived at the
> place and saw him, passed by on the other side."
> (Luke 10:31–32)

As a master storyteller drawing his audience into the heart of God and his kingdom, Jesus mentioned that the priest and Levite had come down from Jerusalem. This detail means that they had already performed their temple duties, so they would not have been in violation of Numbers 19:11, which said: "The person who touches any human corpse will be unclean for seven days."

The priest and the Levite in the parable serve as a symbol of the Jewish religious establishment of Jesus' day. These figures walk past a Jewish man in desperate need of help. Isn't it ironic that the priest and the Levite had been in the temple, the sacred place where heaven and earth meet, where they performed sacrifices, and where they worshiped God, yet they walked right past a person in need of help?

The equivalent in today's culture would be going to Sunday worship and hearing the preaching of the gospel, singing songs, receiving the Lord's Supper, fellowshipping, and baptizing new believers, and then *walking right past a person in dire need*. Yet we are guilty of doing exactly that! What we miss is that our relationship with God should always cause us to *extend mercy to our neighbors in need*. Love is not walking past pain. Love is when mercy meets human pain and suffering.

Paul says, "What matters is faith working through love" (Gal. 5:6), and James writes, "Indeed, if you fulfill the royal law prescribed in the Scripture, love your neighbor as yourself, you are doing well" (James 2:8). Our capacity to love God by loving people is the overflow of the Spirit's power in us.

A story is made great when the storyteller surprises you with an element that is inconceivable. What Jesus says next would have floored his Jewish audience. He informs them that a hated Samaritan, an enemy of the Jewish people, was journeying on the same road, saw the beaten, bloodied Jewish man, and had compassion for him.

Saying a Samaritan would have compassion on a Jewish man is like saying circles are square. This paradigm seemed impossible in the historical context.

> "But a Samaritan on his journey came up to him, and when he saw the man, he had compassion. He went over to him and bandaged his wounds, pouring on olive oil and wine. Then he put him on his own animal, brought him to an inn, and took care of him. The next day he took out two denarii, gave them to the innkeeper, and said, 'Take care of him. When I come back I'll reimburse you for whatever extra you spend.'" (Luke 10:33–35)

The Samaritan teaches us a lot about mercy. First, *mercy isn't afraid to touch human suffering.* The Samaritan, unlike the Jewish religious leaders, did not avoid the bloodied, beaten man. Rather, he entered his suffering, which was a result of sin that was perpetrated against him. He touched this man's hurt with his own hands. Likewise, on the cross, Jesus touched human suffering and sin, and he took the sins of the world upon himself.

> Yet he himself bore our sicknesses,
> and he carried our pains;
> but we in turn regarded him stricken,
> struck down by God, and afflicted.
> But he was pierced because of our rebellion,
> crushed because of our iniquities;
> punishment for our peace was on him,
> and we are healed by his wounds.
> We all went astray like sheep;
> we all have turned to our own way;
> and the LORD has punished him
> for the iniquity of us all. (Isa. 53:4–6)

Second, *mercy is not afraid to cross ethnic, cultural, and religious barriers.* The very thought of a Samaritan being the hero of the story would have insulted Jewish hearers. During the first-century Second Temple Jewish world, Jews and Samaritans were bitter enemies. Ethnically, Jews considered Samaritans unclean Gentiles because they were a mixture of Jewish and Gentile (pagan) blood. Samaritans didn't think too highly of the Jews either. Culturally, they saw life from vastly different perspectives. There was a great deal of fear and suspicion between the groups. Just like in today's world, a lack of proximity to each other created fear and distrust. They were also at odds from a religious perspective. They were at odds from a cultural perspective. They were at odds in every way imaginable.

As the story continues, the Samaritan man was moved by compassion for the beaten and bloodied Jewish man. He does the unthinkable as mercy moves him across racial, cultural, and religious barriers. Mercy loves people across these barriers because God loves people. Likewise, the cross of Jesus not only forgives our sins, but it also crucifies the various boundaries that separate us. On the cross, the blood of Jesus makes a new ethnic group of people, comprised of all ethnic groups, called the church. *Grace* literally creates a new race.

> But now in Christ Jesus, you who were far away have been brought near by the blood of Christ. For he is our peace, who made both groups one and tore down the dividing wall of hostility. In his flesh, he made of no effect the law consisting of commands and expressed in regulations, so that he might create in himself one new man from the two, resulting in peace. He did this so that he might reconcile both to God in one body through the cross by which he put the hostility to death. (Eph. 2:13–16)

> But you are a chosen race, a royal priesthood, a holy nation, a people for his possession, so that you may proclaim the praises of the one who

called you out of darkness into his marvelous
light. (1 Pet. 2:9)

The apostle Peter uses the term "chosen race," a term that was
first used to describe Israel as God's people with God's mission. He
now assigns it to those who are in Christ—the church. God's new
race (ethnicity) is birthed through the life, death, and resurrection
of Jesus. The early church father Clement of Alexandria called the
Church, the "Third Race"[2] to describe the new multiethnic people
of God.

Of all the people on earth, the Church of Jesus Christ should
be the most unified across ethnic lines because we share Jesus'
bloodline. We are objectively reconciled; we should, therefore, pursue reconciled lives. Grace creates a new race of brothers and sisters
who are called "to live in harmony with one another, according to
Christ Jesus, so that you may glorify the God and Father of our
Lord Jesus Christ with one mind and one voice" (Rom. 15:5–6).
Imagine how different our communities, nations, and world would
be if we walked in the mercy and unity of Jesus.

Third, *mercy costs us something.* Helping those in need isn't
free. The merciful Samaritan wrapped the beaten man's wounds,
pouring oil and wine on them. Bandages, oil, and wine cost money.
The wine was for killing infections, and the oil was for softening
the skin. Then he put the man on his animal and paid for him to
stay at an inn and be taken care of, which also cost money. In all
he spent "two denarii" to help the injured Jewish man.[3] Moved by
compassion, the Samaritan spent fourteen days' worth of wages on
room and board for a man who was supposed to be an enemy. This
act of mercy echoes Jesus' instructions to his disciples:

> "But I tell you, love your enemies and pray for
> those who persecute you, so that you may be chil-
> dren of your Father in heaven. . . . For if you love
> those who love you, what reward will you have?
> Don't even the tax collectors do the same? And
> if you greet only your brothers and sisters, what
> are you doing out of the ordinary? Don't even the
> Gentiles do the same? Be perfect, therefore, as
> your heavenly Father is perfect." (Matt. 5:44–45a,
> 46–48)

Our love and mercy for our enemies are indications that we are in God's family. Jesus doubles down when he says to love your brothers and sisters is natural, but to love your enemies is super-natural. Pagans love transactionally—"If you do this for me, I'll do this for you." Those who participate in the life of Christ love transformationally—"I will bless you. It is my privilege to serve you, regardless of what I get from it." Transactional love acts to receive. Transformational love acts because it has already received love from Christ.

For so long in American Christianity, I have sensed that we think that if only we believe the right doctrines, we are following Jesus. As a pastor, theologian, and disciple of Jesus, I love doctrine. But doctrine is meant to be lived, not simply studied or talked about. Our confession of "Jesus is Lord" is more than a doctrinal statement; it is an affirmation of the eternal work of God the Holy Spirit through the wondrous achievements of Jesus. As some theologians say, "Orthodoxy (right belief) leads to orthopraxis (right action)." We have faith in Christ, the eternal Son of God who stepped into time and space, was born of the Virgin Mary, clothed himself in humanity, lived and revealed the law perfectly, was tempted in every way that we are, yet did not sin. This Jesus of Nazareth took our place on the cross to free humanity from the prison cell of sin and death. He lay dead for three days in a borrowed tomb, dealing a deathblow to the grave by resurrecting to life as a preview of God's new creation. It is for the Father's glory and by the Spirit's presence that grace and mercy carry us deeper into Jesus' very life, so that *he* can reproduce image-bearers who bear witness to his kingdom on earth.

> TRANSACTIONAL LOVE ACTS TO RECEIVE. TRANSFORMATIONAL LOVE ACTS BECAUSE IT HAS ALREADY RECEIVED LOVE FROM CHRIST.

Loving your brothers and sisters in Christ across cultural, ethnic, and generational lines, and loving your enemies, are the ultimate signposts that God's kingdom has come. That is living the good life in full.

Can you imagine how different the world would be?

Time to Grow

As a father, one of my great joys is watching my children mature. It's so beautiful. God experiences happiness as we mature also. When Jesus calls us to be perfect as our Father in heaven is perfect (Matt. 5:48), the term "perfect" (*téleios*) in this context means to be mature or whole. As we participate in the life of Christ, we mature in our capacity to love our enemies, thus reflecting that we belong to our Father in heaven. If we want to know our level of maturity, we should ask ourselves how much we love those who are hard to love.

Who is your greatest enemy?

Who has hurt you the most?

How do you feel about those who are on the opposite end of the political spectrum from your position?

What people group of a different ethnicity or socioeconomic status do you hold ill will toward?

When we harbor ill will, unforgiveness, and prejudice toward others, we erode our own humanity. In denigrating the image of God in others, we damage it in ourselves. So how do we love our enemies? I have found that the more I think about how Jesus loved me and moved toward me in mercy, forgiveness, and reconciliation even though I was his enemy, I ask myself, *How can I not do likewise?*

> For if, while we were enemies, we were reconciled to God through the death of his Son, then how much more, having been reconciled, will we be saved by his life. And not only that, but we also rejoice in God through our Lord Jesus Christ, through whom we have now received this reconciliation. (Rom. 5:10–11)

I had to deal with this, and still continue to: If Jesus can love me, an enemy, with such grace that he went to the cross, with such mercy that he endured the wrath of God against sin, how can I not learn and allow the Spirit of God to empower me to love my enemies? Are we Christians in America known for loving our enemies, or are we known for our politics and culture wars? The priest and Levite were religiously, politically, ethnically, and culturally united to the Jewish man lying half dead on the side of the road, yet they walked past him. But the Samaritan, who had nothing in common with the Jewish man except humanity, helped him.

Is getting past fear of the "other" easy? No.

Is walking through pain caused by an enemy easy? No.

Is honestly confessing your prejudices easy? No.

Is forgiving someone who has used racial slurs against you easy? No.

Was going to the cross easy for Jesus? No.

But the cross is the doorway to a new way to be human. It's as if Jesus were saying, "This Samaritan is what a human being looks like." In this story the Samaritan, according to the expert of the law, would have not been a son of God, yet the Samaritan is reflecting what it means to be a son of God. As Israel's Messiah and king, Jesus is showing that God's people would now include not only Jews, but all sorts of non-Jews, just as God promised to Abraham long ago (Gal. 3:8).

Let's Move Beyond Tolerance

Tolerance is extolled as one of the greatest virtues in our society. But is mere tolerance really good enough? Would you feel appreciated if someone said to you, "I tolerate you"? Of course not.

We must move beyond tolerance to love. To tolerate another human is to view them in a subhuman way, but to love someone is first to imagine them as God sees them. If you want to know how God sees people, look at the cross.

> But we do see Jesus—made lower than the angels
> for a short time so that by God's grace he might
> taste death for everyone—crowned with glory and
> honor because he suffered death. (Heb. 2:9)

Loving people doesn't require that we accept everything they do. It simply requires that we see people as God sees them—loved, valuable, and redeemable—and then treat them that way. I have yet to hear someone say they came to faith in Christ because a follower of Jesus was a mean-spirited jerk. It is God's kindness that leads people into his kingdom (Rom. 2:4).

As Jesus comes to the startling, paradigm-shifting end of his story, I'm reminded of how Jesus spent what was most precious on us. He spent his life on us so he could bandage us in his righteousness, pour out the power of the Holy Spirit like oil on us, and cover us in his "blood of the covenant, which is poured out for many for the forgiveness of sins" like the wine in the story (Matt. 26:28). Jesus was the only one rich enough to pay our sin debt so we could enter his kingdom.

> For you know that you were redeemed from your empty way of life inherited from your fathers, not with perishable things like silver or gold, but with the precious blood of Christ, like that of an unblemished and spotless lamb. (1 Pet. 1:18–19)

After Jesus eluded the lawyer's trap, he laid out his own, asking the lawyer:

> "Which of these three do you think proved to be a neighbor to the man who fell into the hands of the robbers?"
> "The one who showed mercy to him," he said.
> Then Jesus told him, "Go and do the same." (Luke 10:36–37)

What if we all showed a little more mercy to those around us? What if we moved beyond tolerance to love? To costly, self-sacrificial, Christlike love?

Happy are the merciful, for they will receive mercy.

> But God, who is rich in mercy, because of his great love that he had for us, made us alive with Christ even though we were dead in trespasses. You are saved by grace! (Eph. 2:4–5)

——————— Marinate on This ———————

Prayer

Father,

As I count all the ways you have been merciful to me, may I be forever grateful. May my heart sing songs of thankfulness to you all the days of my life and on into eternity.

Lord Jesus,

Your mercy met me in my dark hour and carried me to the light of your love and kingdom. May my heart forever sing songs of appreciation to you all the days of my life and on into eternity.

Holy Spirit,

Considering the mercy that the Father and Son have showered upon me as a gift of grace and unfailing love, may my life be a song called mercy. May my response to your mercy be a life of mercy.

In the name of the One who is mercy, amen.

Questions for Reflection

1. Jesus shares his mercy with us so that we may become merciful. How have you seen mercy at work in your life?

2. Who is your neighbor? Take a moment to reflect on this important question. Maybe it is someone with the opposite political views from yours. Maybe it is someone from another country who is attempting to immigrate to your country. Maybe it is the troublemaker from the "bad" neighborhood. Maybe it is the snooty mom on the PTA. Who is your neighbor and how can you show them mercy?

3. Mercy isn't afraid to touch human suffering. Who around you is suffering? How can you enter into their suffering and show them love?

4. How can you reach across cultural, ethnic, and generational lines to love someone who is different from you? What opportunities can you take advantage of?

5. How does God see people? How can you transform the way you see people to align with the way God sees them?

Things to Remember

1. As the final Passover Lamb, Jesus shed his blood to free us from being held hostage to sin, death, and evil.

2. Mercy himself comes to show a better way to be human. Mercy is not something God does, it's who he is.

3. Mercy is God presenting himself to us in the midst of our mess.

4. We only know Jesus is merciful because he pursues us.

5. Jesus fights for us even when we're fighting against him.

6. Mercy is not afraid to cross ethnic, cultural, and religious barriers.

7. The cross of Jesus not only forgives our sins, but it also crucifies the various boundaries that separate us.

8. Mercy costs us something.

CHAPTER 7

Happy Are the Pure

"Blessed are the pure in heart,
for they will see God." (Matthew 5:8)

On the side of a hill overlooking the Sea of Galilee, Jesus continued his teaching on human happiness. "Blessed are the pure in heart," he said, "for they will see God" (Matt. 5:8). Jesus' first-century Second Temple Jewish audience would have known that the only way to see God was in the temple, in the *Shekinah* glory in the Holy of Holies. Only the high priest could enter there, and only once a year. He would be required to have perfect ritual purity and cleanliness.

As Jews, they would have known that no one can see God and live (Exod. 33:20). The eternal Son of God clothed himself in humanity so we could see him. Jesus, the Messiah, comes as the bearer of the new covenant; he wants to go beyond external purity and cleanliness laws to something deeper. The prophet Jeremiah expresses what Jesus means about being pure in heart: "I will put my teaching within them and write it on their hearts. I will be their God, and they will be my people" (Jer. 31:33). For a people grounded in the Hebrew Scriptures, *the thought of being pure in heart always depended on God making his people clean and pure.* There isn't enough soap in the world to clean us. The psalmist asks a great question:

> Who may ascend the mountain of the LORD?
> Who may stand in his holy place?
> The one who has clean hands and a pure heart,
> who has not appealed to what is false,
> and who has not sworn deceitfully.
> (Ps. 24:3–4)

Which one among the sons and daughters of men can stand the scrutiny of this test? Which offspring of Adam has clean hands and a pure heart? There is no one (Rom. 3:10). Therefore Jesus came among us to be the only One, the One who could say with integrity, "My hands are clean and my heart is pure." The eternal Son of God came to stand in our stead at every single level of our existence.

Because we are impure, he came to be our purity.

Because we are unclean, he came to be our cleanliness.

Because we are full of deceit, he came to be our truth.

Because we are unholy, he came to be our holiness.

All that he is, we are. By the Holy Spirit, when we believe in Christ for salvation, we are grafted into him; because we are *in Christ*, what is true of him becomes true of us. He became like us so we can become like him. This is the good life.

> For by that one offering he forever made perfect
> those who are being made holy. (Heb. 10:14 NLT)

All that we could never be or measure up to, Jesus is for us. As our representative, Jesus is our "enough," our "measuring up." Jesus, the Second Person of the Great I AM, is everything that we need to have the good life. Without his grace, we can never be pure of heart and clean enough to see God. The God who requires purity and cleanliness becomes the sacrifice that makes the impure pure and the unclean clean.

Often our lack of happiness is interwoven with the lack of happiness that we have in ourselves. For whatever reason—maybe something awful was done to us or we did something awful, or we just feel unworthy, unknown, or unloved—we constantly feel a nagging sense of sadness rooted in our own inadequacy. Maybe you feel like you should be at a different place in your life by now? It's hard to be happy if you think that you suck.

As we come to embrace that all of who Jesus is, is all of who we are, we will begin to see ourselves the way God sees us.

Our union in Christ is our reunion as the Father's beloved children.

God's children are worthy.

God's children are known.

God's children are loved.

All this is true because the Son of God created sons and daughters of God who are now eternally united to him. His sacred status is our sacred status. We are his and he is ours. Our lives are forever-and-ever engrafted into his, so much so that God the Father sees us as him.

Do you find this hard to believe? Good! I hope you do. Grace, when it's really grace, seems too good to be true because it's too great for our minds to conceive. Nevertheless, it *is* true.

For if we have been united with him in the likeness of his death, we will certainly also be in the likeness of his resurrection. (Rom. 6:5)

I have been crucified with Christ, and I no longer live, but Christ lives in me. The life I now live in the body, I live by faith in the Son of God, who loved me and gave himself for me. (Gal. 2:20)

Higher

Who are the one or two people you would be the most overwhelmed to meet? Who is that person that would just put you in straight-up "I am a twelve-year-old girl losing my mind at a Justin Bieber concert" mode? If you are into tech, maybe your person is the iconic genius, Steve Jobs? Maybe it's a former president like Abraham Lincoln or John F. Kennedy? Maybe that person is a movie star or musician. I'm sure my grandmother would have fainted if she met Elvis Presley. The higher you see someone, the more you respect, admire, and honor him or her—and the more likely you are to lose your mind if you meet them.

> **GRACE, WHEN IT'S REALLY GRACE, SEEMS TOO GOOD TO BE TRUE BECAUSE IT'S TOO GREAT FOR OUR MINDS TO CONCEIVE.**

Here's a story about the time I was starstruck.

In 1984, I was a seventh-grader who experienced the wonder and joy of going to a video game arcade, like the kids in the Netflix blockbuster show *Stranger Things* and a San Antonio Spurs versus

LA Lakers basketball game at the old HemisFair Arena in downtown San Antonio. After my mom dropped off my friend and me at the arena, she said, "Go to the Marriott Hotel, that's where the Lakers will be after game." To this day, I have no clue how she knew the Lakers would be there. At the end of the game, which the Spurs won, my friend and I ran over to the Marriott. After just a few minutes, the Lakers players started showing up. I remember the great Bob McAdoo was still wearing his warm-ups as he walked somberly toward the Marriott. I touched him on the back of his right shoulder.

Next, Gene Banks, a star player for the Spurs showed up. I ran over and gave him a high-five and told him, "Great game!" A few more moments went by and the seven-foot-two-inch Kareem Abdul Jabbar came. I ran over to him and he shook my hand. I was so pumped. But then, with a massive group of people surrounding him, Magic Johnson walked by me . . . and I froze. I was so in awe I couldn't move. Time stood still. It was like he was walking in slow motion. His trademark "Magic Johnson Smile" was on full display lighting up the night. It was a surreal moment.

And then he was gone.

I missed my chance to shake his hand as he entered the hotel. But the feeling I got when he walked past me has never left.

So, what's my point in telling you my fanboy story? First, the higher we view someone, the more we will allow them to direct and shape our lives.

That which we admire, we desire to become like.

That which we esteem, we are willing to glean from.

That which we elevate, we try to emulate.

This is simply called worship.

High Praise = High God

The higher we view God, the more we will praise and obey him because of who he is and what he has accomplished for us. A low view of God produces a low response to God. Why would we want to follow and obey a puny, weak god? Think about it: How do you treat things that you do not place a high value on? Let's get deeper: How do you value and treat people who are considered of a lower status than you? At Transformation Church, our first value is "A High and Lofty View of God." This value states:

> We are committed, through the Spirit's enabling power, to teach a high and lofty view of the Father, the Son, and the Holy Spirit. All our actions, teaching, prayer, mission, and spiritual transformation will be driven by our view of God.[1]

Only a great God is worthy of great worship. The apostle John helps us see Jesus' greatness,

> And they sang a new song:
> You are worthy to take the scroll
> and to open its seals,
> because you were slaughtered,
> and you purchased people for God by your
> blood
> from every tribe and language and people
> and nation.
> You made them a kingdom and priests to
> our God,
> and they will reign on the earth.

Then I looked and heard the voice of many angels
around the throne, and also of the living creatures
and of the elders. Their number was countless
thousands, plus thousands of thousands. They
said with a loud voice,
> Worthy is the Lamb who was slaughtered
> to receive power and riches and wisdom and
> strength
> and honor and glory and blessing!

I heard every creature in heaven, on earth, under
the earth, on the sea, and everything in them say,
> Blessing and honor and glory and power be
> to the one seated on the throne, and to the
> Lamb, forever and ever! (Rev. 5:9–13)

This Jesus is the King of glory who, with the Father and the Spirit, is worthy of our admiration and worship. This Jesus is the one who can transform us to reflect his radiance and beauty into the world. This is the good life.

As we begin to behold God and how epic he is, we will allow him to take hold of our lives so we can thrive as children of his kingdom. The greatest thought we could ever conceive is of God himself, yet our grandest and most majestic thoughts don't even scratch the surface of how beautifully infinite God actually is.

Several years ago, my family and I went to Copenhagen, Denmark. My wife's family immigrated from Denmark in the late 1800s, so our kids wanted to learn about their heritage from that side of the family. As we bounced around Copenhagen like wide-eyed children, we found ourselves at the SMK-National Gallery of

Denmark. Many of the paintings moved us to silence as the vivid beauty slowed our thoughts and attuned our hearts. Gazing at beauty operates beyond linear thinking and makes its way into the soul, igniting our imagination.

Beholding beauty transforms us.

Beholding beauty rearranges the mental furniture of our minds.

Beholding beauty makes us want to be beautiful.

As the Spirit of God whispers our names and calls us to Jesus,

BEHOLDING BEAUTY REARRANGES THE MENTAL FURNITURE OF OUR MINDS.

God is saying, "Come, see, and experience how beautiful I AM. Let my beauty cover your scars and flaws." King David, thousands of years ago, echoed this invitation:

> I have asked one thing from the LORD;
> it is what I desire:
> to dwell in the house of the LORD
> all the days of my life,
> gazing on the beauty of the LORD
> and seeking him in his temple. (Ps. 27:4)

In an act of grace—not of compulsion, but out of unending love—God reveals himself to us in the person of Jesus of Nazareth.

The eternal Son of God made the unknowable knowable.

Jesus made the invisible visible.

The Messiah made the unreachable reachable.

> No one has ever seen God. The one and only Son,
> who is himself God and is at the Father's side—he
> has revealed him. (John 1:18)

He is the image of the invisible God. (Col. 1:15a)

The glory of God, which means the fullness of his immense being, is revealed in the face of Jesus. Paul the apostle said it this way: "For God who said, 'Let light shine out of darkness,' has shone in our hearts to give the light of the knowledge of God's glory in the face of Jesus Christ" (2 Cor. 4:6). If we ever want to know what God is like, all we need to do is look at Jesus. Jesus is the "radiance of God's glory and the exact expression of his nature, sustaining all things by his powerful word" (Heb. 1:3a). To look

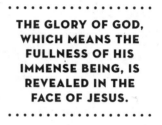

THE GLORY OF GOD, WHICH MEANS THE FULLNESS OF HIS IMMENSE BEING, IS REVEALED IN THE FACE OF JESUS.

at Jesus is to look at God looking in a mirror. God in his beauty is invisible, so he made himself visible in Jesus of Nazareth.

Self-Help Coach Jesus

As an American follower of Jesus, I often feel that in some of the most influential streams of Christianity, Jesus is presented not as the radiance of the eternal God, but as a twenty-first-century self-help coach.

This Jesus gives good advice on how to raise kids, how to find a life partner, and how to solve your problems by providing you with five easy steps to success. This Jesus is really obsessed with you being successful and having an upper-middle-class life. He doesn't give much attention to you becoming holy or learning a theology of suffering or lament. He is also good at helping you find and fulfill your dreams. All you need is faith, and your faith will release *him to do what you want him to do* in your life.

It's like you have faith in your faith, not actual faith in Jesus and his will for your life. This Jesus isn't Lord. He isn't Jewish. He isn't the New Passover Lamb. He has been stripped out of history and plopped right into the mainstream of American materialistic culture. This Jesus doesn't talk about racial problems or poverty or misogyny or injustice. He stays away from controversial issues—for goodness' sake, people may get uncomfortable! Self-Help Coach Jesus is also good at giving forgiveness, not for sins, but for not reaching your potential. And he doesn't require obedience to overcome sin on your part. This Self-help Coach Jesus would never say:

> "If anyone wants to follow after me, let him deny himself, take up his cross daily, and follow me. For whoever wants to save his life will lose it, but whoever loses his life because of me will save it. For what does it benefit someone if he gains the whole world, and yet loses or forfeits himself? For whoever is ashamed of me and my words, the Son of Man will be ashamed of him when he comes in his glory and that of the Father and the holy angels." (Luke 9:23–26)

I hope you can see through my frustration to see my heart. Jesus is the human face of God. The greater we see him, the more he will influence us, *because we are only capable of worshiping someone who we deem greater than we are.*

> Our Lord and God,
> you are worthy to receive
> glory and honor and power,

because you have created all things,
and by your will
they exist and were created. (Rev. 4:11)

New and Better

Becoming clean and pure enough to see God for Jesus' original Jewish audience was about a unique, life-giving story with which the nation of Israel was entrusted: the one true God who longs and loves to be with his children, the temple where God's presence dwelt, the high priest who stood between God and man as a mediator, and the unblemished Lamb who acted as a blood sacrifice that atoned the people's sin. This atonement created an exodus people who journeyed toward the promised land. God's children were a missionary community of light for the Gentiles who were lost in darkness.

"I am the LORD. I have called you
for a righteous purpose,
and I will hold you by your hand.
I will watch over you, and I will appoint you
to be a covenant for the people
and a light to the nations,
in order to open blind eyes,
to bring out prisoners from the dungeon,
and those sitting in darkness from the prison
house.
I am the LORD. That is my name,
and I will not give my glory to another
or my praise to idols. (Isa. 42:6–8)

This unique, life-giving story is a story of a God who desires to have a family. He makes a covenant of love with his beloved people. And this beloved, covenant family would be nourished by the very life of God himself. The worship that was due his name was in response to his grace: "Then God spoke all these words: I am the LORD your God, who brought you out of the land of Egypt, out of the place of slavery" (Exod. 20:1–2). God freed his people from slavery so they could free the Gentiles from slavery to idols. Their primary act of obedience was to love God, themselves, and their neighbors. When Jesus arrived on the landscape of human history, this unique, life-giving story was revealed to have been about him the whole time.

Jesus is every single one of these themes. John writes, "The Word became flesh and dwelt among us. We observed his glory, the glory as the one and only Son from the Father, full of grace and truth. . . . Indeed, we have all received grace upon grace from his fullness" (John 1:14, 16). The Son of God, of very God, became human. The language that John uses to describe Jesus as "dwelling among us" is temple language. The Jewish temple is where the boundaries of heaven and earth collapse into one. In Jesus, heaven and earth walked among us as the new and better temple. In Jesus, he is the new and better high priest, the new and better Passover Lamb who shed his blood to forgive sins, which is another way of saying God's people are free from the bondage of sin, death, and evil (New Exodus). His death and resurrection create a multiethnic family, a worldwide living temple that is on mission declaring his saving acts of grace to all who will hear and believe, as they journey to the new heavens and earth.

JESUS IS THE NEW AND BETTER EVERYTHING.

Jesus is the new and better everything.

Jesus is the pure and clean One who invites us by faith to participate in his purity and cleanliness. It is through his mercy and grace that we can see God.

David, a man who needed to see God after he killed a man and committed adultery, wrote:

> Be gracious to me, God,
> according to your faithful love;
> according to your abundant compassion,
> blot out my rebellion.
> Completely wash away my guilt
> and cleanse me from my sin.
> For I am conscious of my rebellion,
> and my sin is always before me. . . .
> God, create a clean heart for me
> and renew a steadfast spirit within me.
> (Ps. 51:1–3, 10)

His Best > Our Worst

When we give God our worst, he gives us his best. If he didn't, we'd have no hope. Grace stoops down into our situation and has the final word. Here's a story of how God gives us his best even when we give him our worst.

While in Israel, something fascinating happened to me. I saw a boy, who I suspect was about thirteen years old, and a younger girl herding sheep. I walked close to the kids so I could take a picture of them and their sheep. As I steadied my smartphone to take some candid shots, the sheep started to circle me. As the sheep gathered around me, it gave me insight into how God is our shepherd and we are his sheep. It helped me get a sense of what it must have been like for Jesus when he went to the temple and the people gathered around him.

Early in the morning, Jesus went to the temple and people started to flock to him like they were his sheep and he was their shepherd. Like the good shepherd he is, he sat down and began to feed them through his teaching (John 8:2). As he was teaching, the Jewish religious leaders brought a woman to him who had been caught in the act of adultery. Imagine if a video of the darkest, most shameful thing you've ever done was posted on Twitter, Instagram, Snapchat, or YouTube for the world to see. Can you imagine the depth of shame?

Shame causes the deterioration of one's soul. Shame says, "I am what I did." When a person who has been shamed to the magnitude that the woman caught in adultery was, the victim will often project that shame onto others with whom they are in relationship. Shame becomes an engine that recycles abuse. It tells you that you will never be good enough, never measure up.

Just as thunder follows lightning, guilt always follows shame. Guilt says, "I deserve how I feel. I'm guilty."

Shame and guilt are unrelenting abusers that beat us into submission. Have you ever been to a circus? Have you ever noticed how a little chain holds a giant elephant? How does a little chain keep the elephant in bondage? It's able to because the elephant has been trained into submission since it was little, so now it acts according to how it has been treated for so long. Shame and guilt have the same effect on us too. We have all blown it, and the dark powers of evil create strongholds in our lives that beat us into submission. If only the elephant knew how strong, majestic, and beautiful it was, it would break free. If only you, follower of Jesus, knew how strong, majestic, and beautiful you are in Christ, you would break free. Jesus nailed your shame and guilt to the cross; he got off the cross, but they didn't. He cast your sin into his sea of forgotten memory. Every time you try to ask him if he remembers what you did, he responds:

> Who is a God like me,
> forgiving iniquity and passing over rebellion
> for the remnant of my inheritance?
> I do not retain my anger forever,
> because I delight in faithful love.
> I will again have compassion on you;
> I will vanquish your iniquities.
> I will cast all your sins
> into the depths of the sea.
> (Micah 7:18–19, paraphrase)

There is no condemnation for those who belong to Jesus (Rom. 8:1). God delights in giving us mercy and compassion! Whatever you or I have ever done cannot defeat the God who delights in showering us with mercy and compassion. Condemnation, shame, and guilt don't stand a chance under the weight of the cross! Shame and guilt may try to get in the ring and box Jesus, but they are knocked out every single time. Jesus is undefeated. He's our champion. He's mighty to save. The only things condemned are your shame and guilt. They are condemned to the bottom of the ocean. So, let's stop putting on our scuba gear and revisiting what God has forgotten and buried. Let's stay on the beach of his grace, soak in his *Son-rays* of mercy, and sip on some ice-cold compassion.

Back to the story. Often when I read the story of the woman caught in adultery, I wonder, *Where is the man who was having sex with the woman?*

Did the religious leaders let the man run away so he could escape public shame?

Was the man having sex with the woman a powerful religious or political figure?

Did the religious leaders set the woman up so they could try to catch Jesus in a trap (John 8:6)? If so, this meant they were willing to hurt this woman for their religious-political motives.

The religious leaders brought the woman to the crowded temple and placed her in the center. All eyes would have been on her. This is an act of abhorrent spiritual abuse. In their quest to destroy Jesus, they were willing to destroy her. They said to Jesus, "This woman was caught in the act of committing adultery. In the law Moses commanded us to stone such women. So what do you say?" (vv. 4–5).

The law of Moses actually said that *both the man and the woman* were to be stoned (Lev. 20:10; Deut. 22:22–24); however, Rome had stripped capital punishment from the Jewish courts, except in the case of a temple violation, which this was not. Here's the trap that they set for Jesus: Would Jesus reject the Jewish law, thus showing that he was not a true rabbi, or would Jesus reject Roman law, which would then give the religious leaders ammunition to tell the Romans that Jesus was an insurrectionist?

When I was growing up in San Antonio, Texas, we called a trap like this a "trick bag." No matter what you do, you lose. What the religious leaders failed to comprehend was that they were playing checkers and Jesus was playing chess. As you'll see, he didn't want to put the religious leaders into a "trick bag" either. He wanted to put them—and the woman caught in adultery—into his kingdom of grace. God's kingdom is big enough for women caught in adultery and for evil religious leaders. All of us are welcome.

Let's look at what grace does in these circumstances:

First, *God gives us his best even though we give him our worst.* The worst is the awful way the religious leaders, who were supposed to represent God, treated this woman. God is "compassionate and gracious . . . slow to anger and abounding in faithful love and truth, maintaining faithful love to a thousand generations, forgiving iniquity, rebellion, and sin" (Exod. 34:6–7a). Because

> **GOD'S KINGDOM IS BIG ENOUGH FOR WOMEN CAUGHT IN ADULTERY AND FOR EVIL RELIGIOUS LEADERS.**

they were not pure in heart, they didn't see God, so they didn't reflect God's faithful love, compassion, and mercy to this woman. But God was gracious—is gracious—to both parties. He wanted to heal both the abusers and the abused, and he still does.

Second, *grace stoops down to pick us up.* As the religious leaders ask Jesus what should happen to the woman, he stoops down to write on the ground with his finger. Many have offered speculations as to what Jesus was writing or why he was doing this. I suspect he was calling to remembrance that it was the finger of God that wrote the law and gave it to Moses:

> On the day of the assembly the LORD gave me the
> two stone tablets, inscribed by God's finger. The

exact words were on them, which the LORD spoke
to you from the fire on the mountain. The LORD
gave me the two stone tablets, the tablets of the
covenant, at the end of the forty days and forty
nights. (Deut. 9:10–11)

The law reveals God's righteousness, and under the weight of
this law, we are all crushed—the woman caught in adultery, the
misguided oppressive religious leaders, those who picked up stones
to harm her, you and me. Jesus is the righteousness of God in
human form because none of us can measure up, so God in Christ
covers us with his righteousness. The God who requires much is
himself the requirement. All those who receive Jesus as their God
and King are given what he accomplished as a gift.

But now, apart from the law, the righteousness
of God has been revealed, attested by the Law
and the Prophets. The righteousness of God is
through faith in Jesus Christ to all who believe,
since there is no distinction. For all have sinned
and fall short of the glory of God. They are justi-
fied freely by his grace through the redemption
that is in Christ Jesus. (Rom. 3:21–24)

The religious leaders were so focused on keeping power and
discrediting Jesus that they lost their way. They could have helped
this poor woman; instead, they almost destroyed her by trying to
destroy Jesus, and all the while, they were destroying themselves.

Third, *grace shows us that no one has the right to throw stones at
another person.* Instead of falling into their trap, Jesus said, "The

one without sin among you should be the first to throw a stone at her" (John 8:7). When we understand the grace of God in Christ Jesus, the very notion of our moral superiority quickly melts. The more we understand God's grace, the more we will remember that we are simply products of God's grace. Grace is the great equalizer because every saint has a past and every sinner has a future. Sadly, many today will stay stuck in their sins by refusing to accept God's grace, thus condemning themselves.

Fourth, *grace empowers us to grow in holiness (love)*. Something beautiful happens when we see God. The people who were going to stone the woman dropped their stones and walked away. The *grace and face* of God in Christ made them aware of their need for grace. They no longer could condemn her without condemning themselves. The more we understand grace, the more we see that it is grace that keeps, nourishes, and sustains us. Then we want to help people when they are caught in the snare of sin. We want to become healers, not condemners.

> Brothers and sisters, if someone is overtaken in any wrongdoing, you who are spiritual, restore such a person with a gentle spirit, watching out for yourselves so that you also won't be tempted. (Gal. 6:1)

As for the woman, she and Jesus are left alone. This section of the once-crowded temple is virtually empty. Jesus asks her where all the people who wanted to stone her to death went. Are they still here? She says they have all dropped their rocks and left. Then Jesus says, "I don't condemn you either. Now go and sin no more" (John 8:10–11, paraphrased).

Grace has a powerful, life-transforming effect. Marinate on the life-altering power of grace.

> For the grace of God has appeared, bringing salvation for all people, instructing us to deny godlessness and worldly lusts and to live in a sensible, righteous, and godly way in the present age, while we wait for the blessed hope, the appearing of the glory of our great God and Savior, Jesus Christ. He gave himself for us to redeem us from all lawlessness and to cleanse for himself a people for his own possession, eager to do good works. (Titus 2:11–14)

Grace is God in Christ being and doing what we can never be and do. As we trust him, he influences our thoughts and actions. His will replaces ours. We grow in loving what he loves. We grow in thinking the way he thinks. We grow in loving his Father and loving people. Grace empowers us to be holy, which is just a term for Christlike. The blood of Jesus cleans us and empowers us to reflect him in the world.

This is what it looks like to see God. The only reason you or I could ever see God is that he gave us a pure and clean heart. Because of his grace to us, we become more gracious and merciful, giving us greater glimpses of his beauty. Pure-hearted people are eager to do good to others.

The good life is looking into the face of Jesus and seeing God. May his beauty make us beautiful.

——————————— Marinate on This ———————————

Prayer

Father,

Thank you for sending Jesus as a gift of grace.

If we want to know what you look like, all we must do is look at him, because he is the human face of your beauty.

Holy Spirit,

Open our eyes so we can see how beautiful Jesus truly is.

May the mere sight of him move us to worship him.

May his life-giving beauty move us to see and experience that we have been clothed in his beauty.

Lord Jesus,

We had no hope of being pure in our heart, so you became our purity.

We had no hope of removing our sin, shame, and guilt.

But you, inspired by love, eternally removed our
sin, our shame, and our guilt by the shedding of
your own blood.

We are pure in heart, and we can see you, God,
only because of you.

May the rest of our lives be a happy response to
this grace that we didn't deserve.

In your name, amen.

Questions for Reflection

1. What is the difference in Self-Help Coach Jesus and the Lord Jesus Christ? Have you encountered this caricature of Jesus? How can we be sure we are following the actual Jesus and not this self-help version?

2. What does it mean to have a high and lofty view of God? Read Revelation 4:11 and allow it to guide your thinking. Why is it important to have a high and lofty view of God?

3. Do you find it difficult to accept the grace God offers to you? To others? How can you embrace grace?

4. Grace is powerful and transforms lives. How has grace transformed your life? How can you be a conduit of transformative grace for others?

5. Is there someone special in your life who has been transformed by grace? How are they different? How has the change in them affected you personally? Are you able to see God through them?

6. Grace empowers us to be holy. How have you grown in holiness since experiencing God's grace?

Things to Remember

1. The higher we view God, the more we will praise and obey him because of who he is and what he has accomplished for us, not what we think he can give us.

2. All that we could never be or measure up to, Jesus is.

3. It's hard to be happy if you think that you suck. As we come to embrace that we, by faith, are all of who Jesus is, we will begin to see ourselves as God sees we are.

4. The greater we see Jesus, the more he will influence us because we are only capable of worshiping someone we deem greater than us.

5. Grace empowers us to grow in holiness.

6. Jesus nailed your shame and guilt to the cross and cast your sin into the sea of his forgotten memory.

7. God delights in giving us mercy and compassion.

CHAPTER 8

Happy Are the Peacemakers

*"Blessed are the peacemakers, for they will
be called sons of God." (Matthew 5:9)*

Rodney King, a victim of police brutality, said, "Can't we all just get along?" Based on an observation of humanity, the answer is, "No, we can't all get along because animosity between people is so strong."

> We can see the animosity between the police and minority communities.

> We can see the animosity between Republicans and Democrats.

> We can see the animosity between different ethnic groups in America.

> We experience animosity in our own families.

And on a global scale, animosity touches every inch of this planet. It's everywhere. And when it's everywhere, it becomes like an airborne disease that we can catch.

It's critical that we are immunized by the gospel of peace. The "gospel of peace" will fortify our hearts against this disease (Eph. 6:15). But before we get to the gospel of peace and how it transforms us into peacemakers, let's make some cultural observations. Just like a good doctor, we must consider the symptoms, do some blood work, and have a spiritual MRI so we can diagnose the illness and heal it.

Peace Seems Like a Good Idea Until . . .

Peace, love, and forgiveness seem like a beautiful idea until we are called upon to be the person who jumps between coworkers who are so toxic their poison is spreading like Ebola, infecting and killing the workplace culture. A bad work culture has negative effects on the people trapped in it. One psychotherapist writes, "Workplace toxicity leads to adverse effects in part by stimulating people to ruminate on their negative work experiences."[1] Twenty years of research have shown that a toxic work environment increases "depression, substance use, and health issues among employees."[2] An unhealthy work environment leads to decreased work productivity, low employee commitment, and high employee turnover.[3] Toxic work environments hurt people and business.

The dark powers of evil have one goal—"to steal and kill and destroy" (John 10:10). Think about how much time we spend at work. If that time is toxic, imagine how much harm dark powers are unleashing on people. An unhealthy work environment leads to unhealthy people, who infect their spouses, children, and friends.

The idea of peace is gorgeous until someone offends you and you have to be the one who walks across the hot coals of fear, anger, and frustration to rehab and restore the relationship. The Mayo Clinic writes, "Letting go of grudges and bitterness can make way for improved health and peace of mind. Forgiveness can lead to healthier relationships, improved mental health, less anxiety, stress and hostility, lower blood pressure, fewer symptoms of depression, a stronger immune system, improved heart health, improved self-esteem."[4] Despite the benefits of being a peacemaker, which entail forgiveness, patience, grace, and humility, we often choose not to engage in reconciliation and forgiveness. It just seems too hard for us to eat that slice of humble pie. Unfortunately, our pride that prevents us from pursuing reconciliation will imprison us in a cage of mental, physical, and spiritual illness. And like a virus that causes sickness, the toxins will spread to those we are in relationship with.

Have you ever noticed that when you spend time with negative, toxic people, you find yourself being more pessimistic? Research shows that a small amount of negative brain activity has the potential to weaken our immune systems, making us susceptible to sickness, and could cause a heart attack or a stroke.[5] If we choose not to be peacemakers, we take our lack of peace with us into future relationships. Remember, wherever we go, we take ourselves along. We can only fake being emotionally and spiritually healthy for so long. Eventually, who we truly are is revealed. Here's what happens when we are caught in the clenched fist of unforgiveness:[6]

- We bring anger and bitterness into every relationship and new experience.
- We become so wrapped up in the past that we can't enjoy the present; so wrapped up in what's wrong that we can't enjoy what's right.

- We become depressed or anxious.
- We feel that our lives lack meaning or purpose, or that we're at odds with our spiritual
  beliefs.
- We lose valuable and enriching connected-
  ness with others.

Perhaps my talk of "dark powers" isn't your thing. In the age of scientific enlightenment, if we can't observe something with our five senses, we tend to be skeptical of it. Be careful playing that game because there are plenty of things that we believe that go beyond the ability of the scientific method to measure, such as love, morality, and beauty. The dark powers *do not want you to believe they exist.* There is an unseen world of light and darkness, and a battle raging between them.

But there is good news. Even though the dark powers are still working, the light has won. Jesus has already dealt a death blow to the darkness.

> [God] has rescued us from the domain of darkness
> and transferred us into the kingdom of the Son he
> loves. In him, we have redemption, the forgiveness
> of sins. (Col. 1:13–14)

Forgiveness of sins is the pathway to peace with God and peace with God's other image-bearers. The apostle Paul, a leading Jewish intellectual with Roman citizenship, wrote these words to bring peace in a first-century, multiethnic, multiclass church that he started in Ephesus (in modern-day Turkey):

Finally, be strengthened by the Lord and by his vast strength. Put on the full armor of God so that you can stand against the schemes of the devil. For our struggle is not against flesh and blood, but against the rulers, against the authorities, against the cosmic powers of this darkness, against evil, spiritual forces in the heavens. (Eph. 6:10–12)

The dominion of darkness does not want us to be peacemakers because evil knows that forgiveness, grace, peace, and love lead to life. The human heart is like a garden that requires cultivation so life can flourish. Peacemaking acts as nourishment to help the human heart grow and bloom. Dark powers are active in perpetuating a culture of division, dissension, and death. They are death-dealers, but Jesus is a hope dealer. Listen to Jesus with the ears of your heart: "A thief comes only to steal and kill and destroy. I have come so that they may have life and have it in abundance" (John 10:10).

> **FORGIVENESS OF SINS IS THE PATHWAY TO PEACE WITH GOD AND PEACE WITH GOD'S OTHER IMAGE-BEARERS.**

Life Reimagined

The Beatitudes are a manifesto of hope that enables humanity to reimagine how beautiful and life-giving our species could be under the rule and reign of King Jesus. He is a wise and good King. One of the greatest gifts that God has given humanity is our imagination.

Before the Wright brothers took flight, they had to imagine it.

Before Muhammad Ali could "float like a butterfly and sting like a bee," he had to imagine it.

Before Leonardo Da Vinci painted the *Mona Lisa*, he had to imagine it.

Before we could experience the good life, Jesus had to capture our imagination by embodying it and teaching it. His life and teaching, along with the life-giving power of God the Holy Spirit, enable us to reimagine the Jesus-way-of-being-human, so we can, in turn, live as citizens of his kingdom.

Peacemakers Are Blessed

As Jesus continued his prescription for happiness, he said, "Blessed are the peacemakers, for they will be called sons of God" (Matt. 5:9). This beatitude is intertwined with hungering and thirsting for righteousness and being merciful (vv. 7–8). Becoming a peacemaker requires that we have first been brought into peace with God through the forgiveness that comes by grace through faith in Jesus. It then comes from the overflow of being empowered by God the Holy Spirit to live a righteous and merciful life in response to the gospel that we have believed. Like a river flooded by pouring rain, we are deluged by God's own life. God's righteousness has always been about embodying God's love, and God's love is always merciful. The good life—a life of happiness—is loving God, self, and all of humanity. In the kingdom of God,

MAKING PEACE IS HARD, HAPPY, GOSPEL-WORK.

there is "righteousness, peace, and joy in the Holy Spirit" (Rom. 14:17). Peace is not passive. It is the intentional act of God in Christ to reconcile us unto himself through the cross, thus enabling us to extend peace to others. Making peace is hard, happy, gospel-work.

John Wesley, one of the founders of Methodism, said these words a few hundred years ago. They were true then, and they are true now:

> God is the joy of his heart and the desire of his soul . . . happy in God, yea, always happy, as having in him a "wellspring of water springing up into everlasting life," and overflow in his soul with peace and joy. . . . True religion, or a heart right with God and man, implies happiness, as well as holiness.[7]

God's kind of happiness is deeper and more satisfying than simply something good happening. The happiness of God is a quiet confidence that enters the arena of life and believes it's going to be okay because my redeemer lives, his redemptive purposes will stand, and I will stand with the one who triumphed over sin and the grave. He works all things "for the good of those who love [him], who are called according to his purpose" (Rom. 8:28).

The happiness of God is like a compass that keeps our bearings straight on the narrow path that leads to life.

The happiness of God is like the North Star because it's found in the unchanging character of our faithful God.

The happiness of God is like a lighthouse that guides sailors back home as they journey the rough seas.

Before we go further, let's remember that the first-century, Greco-Roman world of Jesus was chaotic, violent, and tumultuous. Jewish men were awaiting the Messiah to usher in peace by eradicating the Romans from their homeland, and the Romans believed that the Caesar would usher in peace. Rome's method of ensuring peace was through force and brutality. Also, as I shared earlier, many of the Sadducees and Pharisees had become corrupt. Jesus was a Jewish man under the force of the Roman war machine, and he was a member of the *Anawin*, a poor but devout subset of Jewish people, making him a double minority. Jesus saw and experienced Roman oppression and the hardships of being poor and living on the margins. So when we say that the happiness he taught about was more than the good feeling you get when something nice happens to you, we can know that Jesus meant it. He experienced it constantly.

When Jesus correlated our happiness with being peacemakers in a world of violence, injustice, and hardship, his statement would have been considered radical. Jesus' method of eradicating the Romans from the promised land was not to cast them out with the sword, but to usher them into the peace of God *so they could become peaceful people.* Likewise, his method of transforming the corrupt Jewish religious establishment was by giving them the peace of God *so they could become peaceful people.* For Jesus, seeking vengeance is a tool of the ungodly. The Prince of Peace was sent to a world devoid of peace to create peacemakers.

> Friends, do not avenge yourselves; instead, leave room for God's wrath, because it is written, Vengeance belongs to me; I will repay, says the Lord. But if your enemy is hungry, feed him. If he is thirsty, give him something to drink. For in so doing you will be heaping fiery coals on his head.

> Do not be conquered by evil, but conquer evil
> with good. (Rom. 12:19–21)

God's vengeance is often God leaving people to their own devices after they reject his mercy over and over. The oppressor, the abuser, the liar, the selfish, the corrupt are eaten alive by their thoughts and actions. Willfully, arrogantly living outside of God's grace is like having a spiritual autoimmune disease—you begin to attack yourself.

Family Resemblance

When my children were young, they looked like me. As they have become young adults, they look more like their mother. There is a family resemblance because our children carry our DNA.

Jesus says that those who make peace carry his Father's DNA: "Blessed are the peacemakers, for they will be called sons of God" (Matt. 5:9). Those of us who are united to Christ share in the DNA of God, and peacemaking is a family trait. The phrase *sons of God* is a Hebrew idiom for family resemblance. God the Holy Spirit's primary task is to conform us to the image of Christ Jesus (Rom. 8:29). Before we move on, let's do a self-diagnostic:

1. Would people who know you most intimately say that you are a peacemaker?
2. Would people who read your social media posts say you are a peacemaker?
3. Would people who know you say that you participate in gossip, slander, deception, and lies?

4. How would people who know you say you engage in conflict?

5. How would people say you interact with people on the opposite end of the political spectrum?

6. Would people say you pursue peace amid the racial division in America?

The more we soak in God's peace through Christ, the more forgiving, merciful, kind, and compassionate we will become, because our hard hearts will be softened by his grace. His love draws us deeper into his heart, and we start resembling him as we follow him by faith. Thus, the God of peace will express his peace through us.

Being transformed into the image of Jesus is not automatic. Just as you entered God's kingdom through faith, we grow as God's children by faith. It's often slower and more painful than we would like, but by God's grace, we cooperate with him in the process of becoming more like Jesus.

> Therefore, my dear friends, just as you have always obeyed, so now, not only in my presence but even more in my absence, work out your own salvation with fear and trembling. For it is God who is working in you both to will and to work according to his good purpose. (Phil. 2:12–13)

Upward, Inward, Outward

At the heart of the gospel is that God wants his family back. This reunion is called reconciliation. We have gone astray, detached and dislocated from the Creator. As a result of our cosmic betrayal, we have found ourselves enslaved with no means of escape.

But God, who is rich in mercy, filled with "I-am-coming-to-get-my-kids-kind-of-love," sent Jesus as a peace offering so we can be reconciled to him. At the heart of the gospel is reconciliation.

> For God was pleased to have
> all his fullness dwell in him,
> and through him to reconcile
> everything to himself,
> whether things on earth or things in heaven,
> by making peace
> through his blood, shed on the cross.
> (Col. 1:19–20)

God in Christ brings us near through his shed blood. We are moved from being enemies to family, from foes to friends, from orphans to sons and daughters. Even creation itself will be made new through the shed blood of Jesus. In Jesus, "faithful love and truth will join together; righteousness and peace will embrace" (Ps. 85:10).

Through Jesus, peace himself, "we have been declared righteous by faith, we have peace with God through our Lord Jesus Christ" (Rom. 5:1). God's peace enables us to live out this truth—"If possible, as far as it depends on you, live at peace with everyone"—across ethnic, socioeconomic, and political lines, starting in the household of God, and then to those outside the family of God (Rom. 12:18; Col. 4:5).

But like any gift, we must take hold of it, unwrap it with grateful hearts, and live from it in the way our lungs take in oxygen.

We are forever God's family through the reconciling grace of Jesus. That's the good life!

God's peace and the doctrine of reconciliation are two sides of the same coin: "But he was pierced because of our rebellion, crushed because of our iniquities; punishment for our peace was on him, and we are healed by his wounds" (Isa. 53:5). By grace, we are carried into the community and unity of God. We are eternally friends of God. Since God has made peace with us, we can now make peace with ourselves.

Our fussy souls calm down as we rest in God's grace and forgiveness.

Our anxious hearts rest in knowing that our slate has been wiped clean.

Our hearts find peace because Peace found us and said, "You are no longer an orphan, you are my daughter or my son."

> He predestined us to be adopted as sons through Jesus Christ for himself, according to the good pleasure of his will, to the praise of his glorious grace that he lavished on us in the Beloved One. (Eph. 1:5–6)

The separation between us and God is nailed to the cross and the relationship that God the Father has with God the Son is a gift we now possess. Inwardly, as we steady ourselves in the grip of God's grace, we can begin to love ourselves because our worth is found in the infinite value of Jesus. Our inner peace is shaped, not by external factors, but by the eternal cross of Christ. Marinate on this:

> For if, while we were enemies, we were reconciled to God through the death of his Son, then how much more, having been reconciled, will we be saved by his life. And not only that, but we also rejoice in God through our Lord Jesus Christ, through whom we have now received this reconciliation. (Rom. 5:10–11)

Paul says we also "rejoice" because of the reconciliation we have with God. We are happy because God says we are his friends. We are his children. We are *his*. It's like God is saying, "The wall that divided us—I knocked it down by plunging through it with my Son on the cross. His cross is the bridge that unites us." Happiness is knowing that we are loved by God. Jesus, the Prince of Peace, was the peace offering sent so we could become peacemakers. I want to share a story about how peacemakers make the powers of darkness tremble in fear.

> **HAPPINESS IS KNOWING THAT WE ARE LOVED BY GOD.**

White Supremacy to Christ Supremacy

Thomas Tarrants was a child of the deep South, born and raised in Mobile, Alabama, which had been ethnically segregated since its founding in 1702.[8] He attended church and Sunday school regularly until his teenage years. He was even baptized. As a teenager in the 1960s, he experienced the political, social, and cultural upheaval[9] that was going on in America. This seismic shift made him, and those like him, "anxious about America's survival."[10]

To the horror of many in the South, black Americans were asking for and gaining basic civil rights. At the risk of their lives, many courageous young black and white people staged "sit-ins" in white-only restaurants. Black Americans, many of whom were Christ-followers, demanded that unjust voting obstacles be removed so they could experience their right to vote as American citizens. Their social progress and successes made Thomas want to stand up for "God and country."[11]

As a follower of Jesus, I'm in debt to and thankful for the many black pastors and Christians who led the civil rights movement. My mentor and friend Dr. John Perkins, one of the foremost evangelicals involved in the movement, has inspired me with his passion for the gospel and his love for all people. He writes:

> For too long, many in the Church have argued that unity in the body of Christ across ethnic and class lines is a separate issue from the gospel. There has been the suggestion that we can be reconciled to God without being reconciled to our brothers and sisters in Christ. Scripture doesn't bear that out. We only need to examine what happened when the Church was birthed to see exactly how God intends for this issue of reconciliation within the body of Christ to fall out.[12]

For nearly two thousand years, the church has had a biblical theology that all people are bearers of God's image and that all humans deserve justice. Sadly, that has not often been lived out. In America, many white evangelical Christians sat silently on the sidelines as black Americans and their black Christian brothers and sisters went through police dog attacks, church bombings, lynching, murder, and other forms of terrorism. Others stood in opposition to black people—often their black brothers and sisters in Christ—who attempted to gain basic American freedoms that the Constitution promised them. Historians Thomas Kidd and Barry Hankins summarize this attitude toward the civil rights movement this way: "Typical white Baptists in the South viewed civil rights as at best irrelevant to the Christian faith and at worst a threat to their culture."[13] Let me pause. Many of you at this point might be thinking, *Come on, Derwin, that was in the past.* Friends, if we don't acknowledge and own the past, we are doomed to repeat it. The reason we talk about the ugly past is so that we, the multicolored family of God, can create a beautiful future.

Thomas Tarrants read "white supremacist, anti-Semitic literature that was circuiting at his high school."[14] He was also alienated from his father and emotionally troubled. He says, "All these factors made me a good candidate for radicalization." It was at meetings at his high school that he heard the ideology that black people were inferior "to whites, and that desegregation, by enabling intermarriage, would weaken the white race."[15] Biblically and scientifically, there is only one race: the human race. The human race has different ethnicities.

> *Ethnicity* is biblical (Hebrew: *goy* or *am*; Greek: *ethnos*). Ethnicity is created by God as people groups move together through space and time. Ethnicity is dynamic and developed over long periods of time. It's not about power. It's about group identity, heritage, language, place, and

common group experience. . . . Ethnicity is God's
very good intention for humanity.[16]

But as Thomas fell prey to these radical ideologies, he became
convinced not only that there is more than one race, but that black
Americans are inherently inferior to white Americans. As Thomas
immersed himself in these doctrines of hate, he felt he was a part of
a "holy cause."[17] As he grew closer to his white supremacy community, he grew more distant from his family and friends who would
have challenged and helped him to see he was going down the
wrong path. Eventually, he joined Mississippi's White Knights of
the Ku Klux Klan, "the most violent right-wing terrorist organization in the United States at the time."[18] What happened next is like
something out of a movie. He writes:

> Little did I know that my downward spiral into
> extremist ideology, conspiracy theories, and racial
> and ethnic hatred would culminate in violence
> and death. But it did. Late one sweltering sum-
> mer night, as my accomplice and I attempted to
> plant a bomb at the home of a Jewish business-
> man in Meridian, Mississippi, we were ambushed
> in a police stakeout. My partner, a young female
> school teacher, was killed at the scene. Four blasts
> of a shotgun fire at close range left me critically
> wounded. Doctors told me it would be a miracle
> if I'd lived another forty-five minutes.[19]

He was convicted of the attempted bombing and sentenced
to thirty years in the Mississippi State Penitentiary. After only six

months in prison, Thomas, along with two other inmates, escaped. He intended to continue his terrorist activities. After a few days of being on the run, he and the other inmates were apprehended after a gun battle with authorities. One of the inmates was killed in the shootout. After returning to prison and being placed in a six-by-nine-foot cell in the maximum-security unit, he started to read classical philosophy, which eventually led him to read the New Testament. Thomas especially spent time in the Gospels. He writes,

> As I read the Gospels in my prison cell, my eyes were open in a way that went way beyond simply understanding the words on a page. As the true meaning of God's word became clearer, so did its relevance to me. . . . As this process unfolded, my sins came to mind, one after another. Conviction grew, and with that tears of repentance. I needed God's forgiveness. And I knew it came only through trusting Jesus Christ, who had given his life to pay for my sins. One night I knelt on the concrete floor of my cell and prayed a simple prayer, confessing my sins and asking Jesus to forgive me, take over my life, and do whatever he wanted to do with it.[20]

The next morning, Thomas woke up a transformed man. He had a deep desire to read the Bible. God removed the poisonous hate from his heart, and he began to develop friendships with black inmates. He even became friends with the FBI agent who "orchestrated my initial capture as well as the Jewish lawyer who helped me."[21] After serving eight years in prison, something miraculous happened: he received a parole grant to attend university. After attending university, the next forty years of his life led him first to a campus ministry, then a pastoral ministry in a racially diverse church (including speaking and writing on racial reconciliation), and finally to a long ministry of teaching, discipling, spiritual mentoring, and writing at the C. S. Lewis Institute.

Wow, grace is amazing! Who would have ever thought that a white supremacist terrorist, who tried to blow up a Jewish man, who had two gun battles with authorities, would one day be a peacemaker and champion of ethnic reconciliation for the glory of Jesus? Grace catches us by surprise, doesn't it?

A Theology of Racial (Ethnic) Reconciliation

You've probably noticed that I have written about race, or ethnicity, quite a bit. For some of my white brothers and sisters in Christ, this may be rare, and could even seem like a distraction from gospel. However, this way of thinking is a tool that dark powers use to keep God's people divided, disunified, and disloyal to the gospel. A divided church along ethnic lines loses credibility to a watching world. This segregation diminishes the beauty of the bride of Christ.

What if I told you that talking about ethnicity was quite common in the early church? Even Jesus, the head of the church and a Jew, told his Jewish disciples to go "make disciples of all nations" (*ethnos*) (Matt. 28:19). Can you imagine how difficult this must have been for these disciples when the existence of the Jewish people was threatened by Gentiles (non-Jews) who enslaved them in Egypt, took them captive in Babylon, and were now oppressing them in Israel? It's as if Jesus were saying, "Go to the people who have enslaved and oppressed you and share my gospel with them."

If we, as followers of Jesus, strip the ethnic tension out of the gospel, we will lose much of the power of the gospel.

One of the reasons the early church was able to transform the Roman world was because the resurrected Messiah brought different ethnic groups and classes of people together in unity. Neither the Jewish establishment nor the pagan Romans could believe the unity of Jesus' church.

Research by sociologist Michael Emerson shows that churches that lack ethnic diversity "reproduce inequality, encourage oppression, strengthen racial division, and heighten political separation."[22] As followers of Jesus, when we isolate ourselves in bubbles of homogeneity, we will stay trapped in echo chambers of ignorance. We are sanctified faster in the context of ethnic and social difference. God the Holy Spirit uses our differences to make us more Christlike.

Renowned New Testament scholar Scot McKnight writes:

> The church is God's world-changing social experiment of bringing unlikes and differents to the table to share life with one another as a new kind of family. When this happens, we show the world what love, justice, peace, reconciliation, and life together are designed to be by God. The church is God's show-and-tell for the world to see how God wants us to live as a family.[23]

"Stop Talking about Race!"

A few years ago I preached a sermon on Ephesians 2:8–22 titled "Grace Creates New Race." In my sermon, I said, "You can't spell *grace* without spelling *race*. Because of Jesus' accomplishments, a new race of grace is created. This new humanity is called the church." Early the next week, I received an email requesting that I stop preaching about race (ethnicity). I responded, "Okay, but do you know what you are asking me? If you want me to stop talking about ethnicity when I preach, I have to leave out the fact that Jesus and Paul are Jewish. That Peter was a Jewish man meeting with a Roman named Cornelius. That the Israelites were slaves in Egypt and taken captive by the Babylonians. That the woman at the well was a Samaritan, and the new heavens and new earth will be populated with a redeemed community of people from every nation, tribe, and tongue. Do you want me to leave all of that out?"

Sadly, I didn't get a response back.

The point of my response is that it is impossible to properly interpret the Bible properly without understanding the ethnic conflict of the ancient world of Jesus. I firmly believe the church needs a theology of ethnic reconciliation, which, of course, is the gospel. We need peacemakers who build bridges so the body of Christ can be an ethnically unified family, bearing witness to the world of our love for one another.

Ethnic Peacemaking

I want to share with you how you can become a cross-cultural peacemaker. First, understand that the gospel is about God getting his family back, as he promised to Abraham. Paul writes: "Now the Scripture saw in advance that God would justify the Gentiles by faith and proclaimed the gospel ahead of time to Abraham, saying, All the nations will be blessed through you" (Gal. 3:8). Through the life, death, and resurrection of Jesus, not only are we forgiven, made righteous, regenerated, and indwelt with the Spirit, but we are also adopted into God's transcultural united family. As God's family, we are not color-blind; we are color-blessed. We are a diverse and beautiful community of siblings.

Second, the gospel creates a family of oneness where ethnocentrism, classism, and sexism are crucified by the cross. Paul writes: "For those of you who were baptized into Christ have been clothed with Christ. There is no Jew or Greek,

> **THROUGH THE LIFE, DEATH, AND RESURRECTION OF JESUS, WE ARE ADOPTED INTO GOD'S TRANSCULTURAL UNITED FAMILY.**

slave or free, male and female; since you are all one in Christ Jesus. And if you belong to Christ, then you are Abraham's seed, heirs according to the promise" (Gal. 3:27–29). If we belong to Christ, we are clothed in Christ, and we are the promise that God fulfilled in Christ Jesus. It's hard to look down on someone who is clothed in Christ, just like you are. Our ethnic, class, and gender differences are transformed, so that they are no longer points of division, but points to celebrate. In the gospel, our differences become tools of grace to grow us.

Third, the gospel creates peace and reconciliation between ethnic groups. Paul writes:

> For he is our peace, who made both groups one
> and tore down the dividing wall of hostility. In
> his flesh, he made of no effect the law consisting
> of commands and expressed in regulations, so that
> he might create in himself one new man from the
> two, resulting in peace. He did this so that he
> might reconcile both to God in one body through
> the cross by which he put the hostility to death.
> (Eph. 2:14–16)

As Jesus' multicolored family, our peace with God and one another is secured by him. Grace indeed creates a new ethnicity of "differents."

Fourth, as a result of God's grace, we seek to build intentional relationships with brothers and sisters of different ethnic groups. Because we love our siblings, we cultivate a posture of listening and learning, seeking to understand before being understood. This will require us to "put on compassion, kindness, humility, gentleness, and patience, bearing with one another and forgiving one another if anyone has a grievance against another" (Col. 3:12–13). Robert Jones writes:

> White Americans' notions of race and fairness
> are shaped by their everyday experiences (already
> vastly different from those of African Americans),
> which are reinforced by interactions with neigh-
> bors and friends. . . . Despite the demise of Jim
> Crow laws and race-restrictive housing ordinances
> and the rise of integrated workplaces, white
> Americans' most meaningful relationships are
> almost exclusively with other white people. This

effectively closes the door to interactions with people who might challenge what feels like a natural and "common sense" perspective on the events they see on cable television.[24]

It's time to break bread together, to pull up a chair and get to know people who aren't like us. As we break bread, barriers of separation will be broken down and the new people of God will be built up. Being the lead pastor of an intentionally gospel-shaped, multiethnic church has made me a better human being. It's our differences that make us more like Jesus.

Fifth, if the demographics of where your church is located allow for ethnic diversity, help your church begin to reflect the ethnic diversity of the community. How can you do this?

First, pray for the senior leadership of the church to catch a vision for God's heart concerning the church on earth looking like the church in the new heavens and new earth.

> And they sang a new song:
> You are worthy to take the scroll
> and to open its seals,
> because you were slaughtered,
> and you purchased people
> for God by your blood
> from every tribe and language
> and people and nation.
> You made them a kingdom
> and priests to our God,
> and they will reign on the earth.
> (Rev. 5:9–10)

Second, share with the senior leadership of church the two-day roundtable experience that I, along with my staff, lead churches through called the HD Leader Roundtable. This experience is an opportunity for church leaders from around the country to dig deeper into God's Word together, encourage one another, and learn more about multiethnic church planting and leadership. Roundtable sessions cover theology, vision casting, cross-cultural competency, soul care for leaders, and best practices of a multiethnic church.[25]

Third, pray and ask God the Holy Spirit to connect you with your people of different ethnicities. It is impossible to build a multiethnic church if you are not living a multiethnic life. Who sits around your dinner table? Who are your friends?

Our ethnic unity in Christ is a living portrait of Jesus' gospel. Paul's first-century church in Colossae was comprised of the Jews and non-Jews (which consisted of various Gentiles like barbarians and Scythians, who were considered poor and ignorant), the rich (free), and the poor. This church was at one another's throats. Paul reminded the ethnically diverse church in Colossae the gospel truth that they were "in Christ."

Our in Christ-ness is the glue that holds us together.

Our in Christ-ness defines us, not our ethnicity or social status.

Our in Christ-ness makes us brothers and sisters.

> In Christ there is not Greek and Jew, circumcision and uncircumcision, barbarian, Scythian, slave and free; but Christ is all and in all. (Col. 3:11)

People who do not know Christ want a *demonstration* of the gospel before they get an *explanation* of the gospel. Our togetherness speaks the language of God's love.

Fourth, traveling internationally and experiencing the rich variety of God's people in their contexts are helpful. My Christian brothers and sisters in Kolkata, India, transformed me with their love for Jesus, wisdom, and perseverance. I thought I was going there to make a difference, but God sent me to India so my Indian brothers and sisters could make *me* different.

Meditate on Paul's words and how our cross-cultural unity brings God glory.

> Now may the God who gives endurance and encouragement grant you to live in harmony with one another, according to Christ Jesus, so that you may glorify the God and Father of our Lord Jesus Christ with one mind and one voice. Therefore accept one another, just as Christ also accepted you, to the glory of God. (Rom. 15:5–7)

As you and I engage in peacemaking and building bridges of ethnic reconciliation in the church and outside the church, we will be called sons and daughters of God (Matt. 5:9). Wouldn't it be nice for us as followers of Jesus to be known for making peace? This is the good life.

—————————— Marinate on This ——————————

Prayer

Holy Spirit,

Blow up the doors of my heart so the
peacemaking grace of the Lord Jesus can come in.

Open my mind to the reality that it was his
grace that eternally changed my status from foe
to friend, from enemy to family.

Father,

In Christ, your beloved Son, I am now a child
of yours. I now have your DNA swirling and
pulsating in me and through you.

Jesus, our King,

Release your peacemaking love through me.

May I cast seeds of peace wherever I go so they
can take root, mature, and produce fruit to feed
the world.

In the name of the Father, the Son, and the
Spirit, amen.

Questions to Study

1. Becoming a peacemaker comes from the overflow of being empowered by God the Holy Spirit to live a righteous and merciful life. Is this how you have understood peacemaking in the past? Does this challenge your definition for being a peacemaker?

2. This chapter includes a six-question diagnostic assessment (see pages 169–70). As you read and meditate on those questions, what conclusions do you draw? What are some opportunities for growth that you are able to identify?

3. As a son or daughter of God, peace is now in your DNA. How can you embrace this part of your identity?

4. Racial (ethnic) reconciliation is now possible thanks to the cross of Jesus bringing all nations (ethnos) together. How can you be an agent of reconciliation in your community? How can you begin to build a bridge to unify God's family? How can you be a cross-cultural peacemaker?

5. Are you part of a multiethnic church? What is your experience with the multiethnic church? How can you intentionally seek out relationships with others who are not like you?

Things to Remember

1. Peace, love, and forgiveness seem like beautiful ideas until we are called upon to be peaceful, loving, and forgiving toward those who aren't.

2. Forgiveness of sins is the pathway to peace with God and peace with God's other image-bearers.

3. The Beatitudes are a manifesto of hope that enables humanity to reimagine how beautiful and life-giving our species could be under the rule and reign of King Jesus.

4. Becoming a peacemaker comes from the overflow of being empowered by God the Holy Spirit to live a righteous and merciful life.

5. The good life, a life of happiness, is loving God, self, and all of humanity.

6. One of the reasons why the early church was able to transform the Roman world is because the resurrected Messiah brought different ethnic groups and classes of people together in unity.

CHAPTER 9

Happy Are the Persecuted

*"Blessed are those who are persecuted because of
righteousness, for the kingdom of heaven is theirs."*
(Matthew 5:10)

Do you remember your first day of high school? Scary, right?
I remember feeling like a guppy in the Pacific Ocean. As
a freshman football player, I was training with seniors who looked
like grown men with beards and huge muscles. I barely had hair
under my arms. I was at the bottom of the barrel.

By my senior year, I was a team captain with big muscles (but
still no facial hair—I'm not a hairy dude). Being a team captain
made a huge difference in how I experienced life. I was no longer
on the margins. I was in the middle of the action, influencing and
shaping the team culture.

But that all changed in the summer of 1989 when I was a freshman all over again, beginning my college football career at Brigham
Young University. I was once again a tiny fish in an even bigger
ocean. I was on a team with men who were in their twenties; many
of whom were married with children. I played with a guy who was
twenty-seven with four kids! Over the next three years, I went from
a freshman on the margins to a senior team captain. I was once

again leading and shaping the team culture. My perspective was so much different as a captain with influence than as an unknown freshman on the margins with little to no influence.

So, what's my point? At one time in America, the church was in the center of American life, influencing and shaping society. We were once the seniors, the team captains. This is no longer the case. Now, we're more like unknown freshmen.

Ed Stetzer, the Billy Graham Distinguished Chair of Church, Mission, and Evangelism at Wheaton College, provides us with insight into our post-Christian culture:

> For decades, they say, they have been steadily pushed to the sidelines of American life and have come under attack for their most deeply held beliefs, born of their reading of Scripture and their religious mandate to evangelize. The 1960s ban on prayer in public schools is still a fresh wound. Every legal challenge to a public Nativity scene or Ten Commandments display is another marginalization. They've been "steamrolled," they say, and "misunderstood."[1]

In our post-Christian culture, church attendance is dropping, the rise of those who claim no religious affiliation is rising, and belief in God, reading the Bible, and prayer have been declining for decades. For example, according to one survey, Charlotte, North Carolina, where I live, is rated as the 92nd most post-Christian city in America.[2] Despite Charlotte being called the City of Churches, the church's influence here is vanishing. There is a much larger percentage of people who are not connected to a church than who are.

For many followers of Jesus, this push to the margins, along with the loss of influence and power, is cause for concern.

How do you tell a fish that it lives in water? Water is all the fish knows. The first time a fish learns that it lives in water is when it is taken out of water. The caught fish is disoriented and not sure what to do except flop around in the foreign environment in which it finds itself. The church in America for so long has been like a fish swimming in water. Well, the river has dried up, and we find ourselves disoriented, fearful, and not sure how to live on land.

Here's the good news: we as God's people can not only survive on land; we can thrive. As God's people, the church is adaptable to any environment. In Christ, we are a resilient and remarkable people because our God is resilient and remarkable. As a people being moved to the margins of American society, like missionaries, we must learn to adapt to a post-Christian culture.

How do we as the new people of God in the New Exodus stay faithful to Jesus and his kingdom when the church is no longer at the center of influence, and often our beliefs and presence are not welcomed in the public square?

In the midst of the church being pushed to the margins, I believe our post-Christian culture is a fertile environment for the church in America to experience revival. When I say revival, I do not mean a sweaty tent meeting in a small country town. I mean that we, Jesus' church—that is, his community of siblings—can have a deeper, more faithful experience of what it means to follow him and embody his kingdom on earth as it is in heaven.

> **I BELIEVE OUR POST-CHRISTIAN CULTURE IS A FERTILE ENVIRONMENT FOR THE CHURCH IN AMERICA TO EXPERIENCE REVIVAL.**

Global Persecution

As the church is pushed to the margins of American life, various forms of persecutions will arise. But we must not overstate the issue. The persecution of the church in America is not even comparable to the persecution our siblings are experiencing in some places around the world. Religious freedom globally is under assault daily. Christians in Myanmar are being oppressed and tortured by the country's military government.[3] Our siblings in countries like North Korea, Afghanistan, Somalia, Libya, Pakistan, Sudan, India, and Nigeria, to name a few, are being persecuted with imprisonment, violence, kidnapping, and death.[4]

In this chapter, I will not be addressing the persecution our siblings are experiencing around the world primarily because I do not believe I can speak to it with credibility.[5] The persecution that I will address in this chapter will be the American church's cultural marginalization. I hope to show how we can give faithful witness in this new normal, and how we individually can thrive in seasons of persecution.

Persecution Is Like Fertilizer

Persecution has a way of purifying us. As Christ-followers in America are no longer the center of society, there will be new blessings that arise. James, the half-brother of Jesus, wrote:

> Consider it a great joy, my brothers and sisters,
> whenever you experience various trials, because
> you know that the testing of your faith produces
> endurance. And let endurance have its full effect,

so that you may be mature and complete, lacking
nothing. (James 1:2–4)

James says that trials (*peirasmós*), which can be translated as
persecutions, are used by God to stimulate our growth in endurance, and endurance enhances our capacity for spiritual maturity
as disciples of Jesus. Persecution is like holy fertilizer that sinks into
the soil of our hearts and minds, producing Christlikeness as we
respond to Jesus in faith. Even persecution is redeemable in God's
society.

What the enemy means for evil, God uses to produce good in
our lives. Persecution tests our faith.

Through the history of God's people, he has used testing to
bring the best out of us. For example, God tested Abraham. "'Take
your son,' he said, 'your only son Isaac, whom you love, go to the
land of Moriah, and offer him there as a burnt offering on one of
the mountains I will tell you about'" (Gen. 22:2).

Abraham and his wife Sarah had waited for so long for this
beautiful boy, and now God was asking him to sacrifice him.
Abraham must have been shocked and devastated. But he displayed
faith in God. He believed that somehow God would provide a
sacrifice: "Abraham answered, 'God himself will provide the lamb
for the burnt offering, my son.' Then the two of them walked on
together" (Gen. 22:8).

I suspect the circumstances looked bleak, but Abraham looked
to God. During persecution, we, too, must learn to look at the
God who provides and not our circumstances that often divide our
minds. Here's the rest of the story:

> Then Abraham reached out and took the knife
> to slaughter his son. But the angel of the LORD
> called to him from heaven and said, "Abraham,
> Abraham!" He replied, "Here I am." Then he said,
> "Do not lay a hand on the boy or do anything to
> him. For now I know that you fear God, since
> you have not withheld your only son from me."
> Abraham looked up and saw a ram caught in
> the thicket by its horns. So Abraham went and
> took the ram and offered it as a burnt offering in
> place of his son. And Abraham named that place
> The LORD Will Provide, so today it is said: "It
> will be provided on the LORD's mountain." (Gen.
> 22:10–14)

Just as Abraham was tested, we will be too. God, in his sovereign goodness, will take persecution and shape it to test us, to teach
us how to rely on him for everything we need. This is the good life.
The good life does not try to get even with a society that marginal-
izes us. Why? Because God has our back. Even when it doesn't look
like it, he is in control, and he is the judge, which means we don't
have to respond vindictively to those who treat us like enemies.

I would be remiss if I didn't mention that a few thousand years
later, another son, named Jesus, walked up the same hill and died
on the cross. He asked his Father to remove "this cup" from him,
but his Father told him that he was the sacrifice that would set the
captives free, he was the Lamb of God who was caught in a thicket,
and he was nailed to a cross. When we are persecuted, it's as if we
were drinking from the cup that Christ drank. Paul wrote:

> The Spirit himself testifies together with our spirit
> that we are God's children, and if children, also
> heirs—heirs of God and coheirs with Christ—if
> indeed we suffer with him so that we may also be
> glorified with him. (Rom. 8:16–17)

When we are tested, God produces endurance in us. As we are personally persecuted for following Jesus and remaining true to the way he calls us to live, we learn to endure. Endurance in this context expresses a God-inspired, Christ-exalting determination in the face of adversity. As you view the mercies of God, you find that persecution for the name of Jesus is an honor. Endurance allows us not to grow in bitterness or pettiness, but to be patient with a culture that is fractured and hurt. *The good life is found in becoming who you were meant to be.*

James goes on to say we should consider it "joy" when persecution comes. James is restating Matthew 5:10–11. But this seems insane! Why should we be joyful when persecutions come? We want naturally to do the exact opposite.

Here's why: because the good life is being cultivated in us. The good life is a life in which God orchestrates everything to make us look like the Author of life, King Jesus. The good life is becoming good:

> He gave himself for us to redeem us from all
> lawlessness and to cleanse for himself a people
> for his own possession, eager to do good works.
> (Titus 2:14)

God redeems us with his sin-cleansing blood, making us his own, and out of joyous new hearts, we want to share and be his goodness in the world.

Life on the margins requires a deeper level of understanding of the beauty of our faith, a higher commitment to be the church in the world, and a strong cultivation of discipleship. Living from the center, with its cultural privileges and blind spots, often weakens the church by causing her to drift from her mission. The twenty-first-century church must go back and learn from the first-century church so we can be a faithful church in the present, leading to a better future. By being pushed to the margins, we are being pushed closer to Jesus and his redemptive purposes for our lives.

Back to the Future

Sociologist and comparative religion expert Rodney Stark asks, "How did a tiny and obscure messianic movement from the edge of the Roman Empire dislodge classic paganism and become the most dominant faith of Western Civilization?"[6] The Church—a people from every nation, tribe, and tongue who have been purchased through the shed blood of Jesus—began as a tiny, fringe, marginalized community. What the early church lacked in cultural, political, or economic power, it made up for through the Holy Spirit's power. This new messianic movement, gathered and centered on Jesus and his mission, was a unicorn in the ancient world. Many of the Messiah's earliest followers were ethnically Jewish. But they were rejected by the Jews at large because they worshiped Jesus as Lord (*kurios*), a term that was uniquely used for the one true God of Israel. Christians believe that God is three-in-one, the Trinity.

There is only one God, and he exists as Father, Son, and Holy Spirit. But when the Jewish people heard Christians refer to Jesus as God (the Son), it seemed like a denial of their monotheism. Luke, Paul's Gentile traveling companion, described the Jewish religious establishment's hostile posture toward the apostles and the early church:

> After they ordered them to leave the Sanhedrin, they conferred among themselves, saying, "What should we do with these men? For an obvious sign has been done through them, clear to everyone living in Jerusalem, and we cannot deny it. But so that this does not spread any further among the people, let's threaten them against speaking to anyone in this name again." So they called for them and ordered them not to speak or teach at all in the name of Jesus. Peter and John answered them, "Whether it's right in the sight of God for us to listen to you rather than to God, you decide; for we are unable to stop speaking about what we have seen and heard." After threatening them further, they released them. They found no way to punish them because the people were all giving glory to God over what had been done. For this sign of healing had been performed on a man over forty years old. (Acts 4:15–22)

The Messiah's other followers were Gentiles, non-Jews from all over the ancient world. As a result, many of the Gentiles rejected them because they stopped worshiping idols in the pagan temples, and they also stopped buying idols, which was bad for pagan businesses. Paul described the transformation of the Gentiles who followed Jesus:

> As a result, you became an example to all the believers in Macedonia and Achaia. For the word of the Lord rang out from you, not only in Macedonia and Achaia, but in every place that your faith in God has gone out. Therefore, we don't need to say anything, for they themselves report what kind of reception we had from you: how you turned to God from idols to serve the living and true God and to wait for his Son from heaven, whom he raised from the dead—Jesus, who rescues us from the coming wrath. (1 Thess. 1:7–10)

Through the formation of transcultural Jesus communities, Gentiles were following Jesus and becoming the new people of God at such an exponential rate that businesses that sold items for pagan worship were losing money. This led to a riot in one Gentile city.

> About that time there was a major disturbance about the Way. For a person named Demetrius, a silversmith who made silver shrines of Artemis, provided a great deal of business for the craftsmen. When he had assembled them, as well as the workers engaged in this type of business, he said: "Men, you know that our prosperity is derived from this business. You see and hear that not only in Ephesus, but in almost all of Asia, this

man Paul has persuaded and misled a consider-
able number of people by saying that gods made
by hand are not gods. Not only do we run a risk
that our business may be discredited, but also that
the temple of the great goddess Artemis may be
despised and her magnificence come to the verge
of ruin—the very one all of Asia and the world
worship." (Acts 19:23–27)

This little Jesus movement that existed on the margins of
the Roman Empire with no economic or political power brought
Ephesus to its knees because of the gospel's power.

Persecution, Scattering, and the Growth of Jesus' Church

In Acts 1:8, which provides the geographical outline of Acts:
Jerusalem, chapters 1–7; Judea and Samaria, chapters 8–12; end
of the earth (i.e., Rome), chapters 13–28,[7] Jesus restates the Great
Commission when he tells his disciples, "But you will receive power
when the Holy Spirit has come on you, and you will be my witnesses in Jerusalem, in all Judea and Samaria, and to the end of the
earth" (Acts 1:8). Keep in mind the difficulty of this sacred task;
Jesus is mobilizing his Jewish followers to become missionaries to
those who had oppressed them, those who had nailed their people
to crosses, and those whom the Jews considered unclean. *Go reach
your enemies*, he was telling them. This was hard two thousand years
ago. And it's hard today.

The church in Jerusalem, which was overwhelmingly Jewish,
stayed in Jerusalem and did not go on mission to Judea, Samaria,
and the end of the earth to reach the Gentiles. Our triune God's

love for all of humanity is so epic that since his people did not do Acts 1:8, he allowed Acts 8:1 to happen. It was persecution of his church that moved his people to take his message of redemption to the world. Maybe the Jewish believers were afraid of rejection. Maybe it was the sin of ethnocentrism that kept them from leaving Jerusalem. Question: What's your reason for not sharing the gospel with people who are different from you? Regardless of the reason, the church stayed in Jerusalem. God, in his grace, with his redemptive mission in mind, allowed for persecution to scatter his Jewish children into Gentile regions to fulfill his mandate.

> Saul agreed with putting him to death. On that day a severe persecution broke out against the church in Jerusalem, and all except the apostles were scattered throughout the land of Judea and Samaria. Devout men buried Stephen and mourned deeply over him. Saul, however, was ravaging the church. He would enter house after house, drag off men and women, and put them in prison. So those who were scattered went on their way preaching the word. Philip went down to a city in Samaria and proclaimed the Messiah to them. The crowds were all paying attention to what Philip said, as they listened and saw the signs he was performing. For unclean spirits, crying out with a loud voice, came out of many who were possessed, and many who were paralyzed and lame were healed. So there was great joy in that city. (Acts 8:1–8)

God made a promise to Abraham. He told Abraham, "I am going to give you a beautifully diverse family." This is the good news. Jesus creates a single family out of the people on earth: "Now the Scripture saw in advance that God would justify the Gentiles by faith and proclaimed the gospel ahead of time to Abraham, saying, All the nations will be blessed through you" (Gal. 3:8).

God scattered his Jewish people through persecution so he could gather Gentiles into his family. Look what happened next:

> Now those who had been scattered as a result of the persecution that started because of Stephen made their way as far as Phoenicia, Cyprus, and Antioch, speaking the word to no one except Jews. But there were some of them, men from Cyprus and Cyrene, who came to Antioch and began speaking to the Greeks also, proclaiming the good news about the Lord Jesus. The Lord's hand was with them, and a large number who believed turned to the Lord. News about them reached the church in Jerusalem, and they sent out Barnabas to travel as far as Antioch. When he arrived and saw the grace of God, he was glad and encouraged all of them to remain true to the Lord with devoted hearts, for he was a good man, full of the Holy Spirit and of faith. And large numbers of people were added to the Lord. (Acts 11:19–24)

Within a short three hundred years, this tiny fringe group overwhelmed the Roman Empire with the gospel.

One of my favorite places on earth is the Bitterroot Valley in Western Montana, where my beautiful bride is from. The mountains are breathtaking. Unfortunately, every few years, there is a wildfire that destroys thousands upon thousands of acres of pristine beauty. Sometimes the fires are started by a lightning strike or a camper who didn't put out his fire properly. I've even heard stories of the fires being set on purpose. All it takes is a flash of lightning and a wildfire can start. The early church was a wildfire because God the Holy Spirit used persecution as a flash of lightning to create a spark that led to a flame. China is experiencing the wildfire today, as are parts of Africa. We need a flash of lightning in America to spark a revival.

This holy fire will be one of prayer, ethnic reconciliation, justice, mercy, mission, and holistic discipleship. In our increasingly cynical, lonely, divided post-Christian culture, our life together as the church will be attractive and compelling. The kingdom of God is characterized by righteousness, peace, and joy (Rom. 14:17). This is the good life. A life of righteousness, reconciliation, and joy-generated happiness.

Happy Are the Persecuted

The fires of persecution have a way of burning off the impurities so Jesus can be formed in his people. But if I'm being honest, of all the Beatitudes, this is the one I like least.

Good gracious. Persecution and suffering? These are not fun, nor will they ever be fun. But I have to trust Jesus when I do not understand. Where else can I go? Who else has the words of eternal life but him? No one.

Trust in the LORD with all your heart, and do not rely on your own understanding; in all your ways know him, and he will make your paths straight. (Prov. 3:5–6)

Jesus' last beatitude says:

"Blessed are those who are persecuted because of righteousness, for the kingdom of heaven is theirs. You are blessed when they insult you and persecute you and falsely say every kind of evil against you because of me. Be glad and rejoice, because your reward is great in heaven. For that is how they persecuted the prophets who were before you." (Matt. 5:10–12)

As you decide by faith to pursue the good life and experience the kingdom of God, you will encounter persecution and opposition from the dark powers that rule this present age. At the very least, you will experience internal spiritual persecution as you fight sin and shed the old way of living. But likely, you'll experience some level of it from the outside world too.

Persecution has a way of bullying us into backing down from our destiny as God's royal priests. When we pursue God's righteousness and his kingdom, we will experience backlash at our corporate jobs. We will be mocked and disliked by teammates. When we choose to walk in Jesus' sexual ethic as an act of worship, we will be made fun of or even disliked. When we choose forgiveness over bitterness and love over hate, we will be called soft. When we choose Jesus over political parties, we will be rejected.

When I first became a follower of Jesus, I tried to talk to some of my old teammates about my newfound faith in Christ. One of my close friends said, "Derwin, all you talk about now is Jesus." I thanked him. One of the greatest gifts we will ever receive is being persecuted for Jesus' glory.

Marinate on Paul's words:

> But he said to me, "My grace is sufficient for you, for my power is perfected in weakness." Therefore, I will most gladly boast all the more about my weaknesses, so that Christ's power may reside in me. So I take pleasure in weaknesses, insults, hardships, persecutions, and in difficulties, for the sake of Christ. For when I am weak, then I am strong. (2 Cor. 12:9–10)

Think deeply on what Paul says: "Take pleasure in weaknesses, insults, hardships, persecutions, and in difficulties, for the sake of Christ" (v. 10). Taking pleasure means to be happy. We are to be happy when our weaknesses are revealed, when we are insulted, when we experience hardships, persecutions, and difficulties for Christ's sake. Why? Because in these moments, we rely on the power of Christ that resides in us. We are at our strongest when we are at our weakest.

Jesus is our defense against false accusations.

Jesus is our security when we feel insecure.

Jesus is our strength when we are weak.

Jesus is our "enough" in any season of life.

We are to be happy when our weaknesses are revealed, when we are insulted, when we experience hardships, persecutions, and difficulties for Christ's sake.

When we love with a Jesus-kind-of-love, the religious will persecute us for eating with those they deem unacceptable or irredeemable. When we pursue the righteousness and moral purity called for by the gospel and proclaim that Jesus is the only way to the Father, the irreligious will persecute us and call us self-righteous or narrow-minded. We will be too conservative for the liberals, and we will be too liberal for the conservatives. Love is the language of God's kingdom. Jesus is the rabbi who teaches us how to live his Father's language, and the Spirit empowers us to be living letters that shout from the rooftops, "How great is our God!"

If we follow Jesus' way, we will see persecution.

If we speak Jesus' truth, we will see persecution.

If we live from Jesus' life, we will see persecution.

Jesus was persecuted. All the apostles were persecuted. The early church was persecuted.

And we will be persecuted.

But Jesus makes an astonishing promise: when we are insulted, falsely accused, and persecuted, we should "be glad and rejoice." Why? Because we have an epic reward (Matt. 5:12). The reward is the tri-personal God himself.

We get more of the infinite one. The one who is eternal happiness becomes our happiness. The reward is an inner satisfaction and happiness located in fulfilling God's purpose and bearing witness to his kingdom on earth as it is in heaven.

Handling Persecution

Sometimes it's the people closest to us who doubt us the most. Jesus was moving about saying and doing things that only the Messiah would say and do. He was healing people. He was forgiving people of sins. He was going around saying he was the temple, the living, breathing embodiment of God's presence. The Jewish religious order took note of this young rabbi from Galilee.

One day while they were spying on him, he entered a home to eat, but so many people came, he couldn't eat. At this point, his family was concerned for his mental health: "When his family heard this, they set out to restrain him, because they said, 'He's out of his mind'" (Mark 3:21). This accusation from Jesus' family had to hurt him. Another angle on this story could be that Jesus' family knew he had gotten on the radar of the Jewish religious establishment. Perhaps they were trying to protect him from the powerful Jewish leaders. Jesus was disrupting and wrecking the temple, healing people on the Sabbath, saying that he is the Messiah, and forgiving sins. All these activities were directly tied to the Jewish temple. Jesus' actions were making the temple obsolete, which meant the Jewish religious establishment was becoming obsolete and that would affect their wealth, status, and power. In the ancient world, just like in today's world, wealth, status, and power are the unholy trinity that people will kill for. It was as if Jesus himself were saying, "The temple made with human hands is no longer needed because in me, not only is the temple present among us, but the God who fills the temple with his glory is here too." This is what the apostle John is alluding to when he writes:

The Word became flesh and dwelt among us. We observed his glory, the glory as the one and only Son from the Father, full of grace and truth. (John 1:14)

Nevertheless, his family said he was "out of his mind," and the scribes who journeyed from Jerusalem said, "He is possessed by Beelzebul," and "He drives out demons by the ruler of the demons" (Mark 3:22).

We can learn some lessons from how Christ handled this situation. First, Jesus had *clarity in the chaos*. The scene was wild. People were everywhere. There was shouting. Emotions were running high. Yet Jesus had clarity in the chaos. He clearly and compellingly destroyed the scribe's arguments:

So he summoned them and spoke to them in parables: "How can Satan drive out Satan? If a kingdom is divided against itself, that kingdom cannot stand. If a house is divided against itself, that house cannot stand. And if Satan opposes himself and is divided, he cannot stand but is finished. But no one can enter a strong man's house and plunder his possessions unless he first ties up the strong man. Then he can plunder his house. Truly I tell you, people will be forgiven for all sins and whatever blasphemies they utter. But whoever blasphemes against the Holy Spirit never has forgiveness, but is guilty of an eternal sin"—because they were saying, "He has an unclean spirit." (Mark 3:23–30)

Second, Jesus had clarity in the chaos because *he knew his identity*, which enabled him not to fall prey to deception. As the *true* human, Jesus lived in perfect communion and union with the Father by the Spirit's power. Jesus was utterly reliant on God the Holy Spirit as we are to be: "Truly I tell you, the Son is not able to do anything on his own, but only what he sees the Father doing. For whatever the Father does, the Son likewise does these things" (John 5:19). God the Holy Spirit reminded him that his identity was in being the Father's beloved and that he was pleasing to his Father, not based on what he did but based on his relationship to him.

> And a voice from heaven said: "This is my beloved Son, with whom I am well-pleased." (Matt. 3:17)

> Then a voice came from the cloud, saying: "This is my Son, the Chosen One; listen to him!" (Luke 9:35)

Amid persecution, we must remember that we are united to Jesus, and thus we are God the Father's beloved. Paul writes "to the praise of his glorious grace that he lavished on us in the Beloved One" (Eph. 1:6). Grace is truly this stunning.

Our standing is secure because we stand in Christ.

Our validation is secure because Jesus validated us by his death on the cross.

Our worth is secure because Jesus' worth is given to us.

The more we find ourselves in Christ, the more we can stand in truth and not be swayed by deception.

When we find our identity in the deep love of God, we are secure enough not to allow the chaos to make us unclear as we demonstrate the kingdom of God. Often, in chaos and persecution, followers of Jesus lose their cool because they forget their identity and fall prey to deception. Paul writes, "Act wisely toward outsiders, making the most of the time. Let your speech always be gracious, seasoned with salt, so that you may know how you should answer each person" (Col. 4:5–6). During the chaos, being cool and loving to those who oppose Christ in us are acts of worship that display what heaven looks like on earth.

Third, as we *root ourselves in our identity as the beloved of God,* we can remain gracious and kind even when people are being hostile toward us. I find myself wanting to respond to persecution and false accusations when I forget who I am in Christ. The desire to defend myself is rooted in forgetting that Jesus is my defense. It is also the result of forgetting that people are not the enemy. Our battle "is not against flesh and blood, but against the rulers, against the authorities, against the cosmic powers of this darkness, against evil, spiritual forces in the heavens" (Eph. 6:12). I have to ask the Spirit to help me remember during persecution that:

> Love is patient, love is kind. Love does not envy, is not boastful, is not arrogant, is not rude, is not self-seeking, is not irritable, and does not keep a record of wrongs. Love finds no joy in unrighteousness but rejoices in the truth. It bears all things, believes all things, hopes all things, endures all things. (1 Cor. 13:4–7)

Love is the medicine that cures soul-sickness.
Love is a weapon that we wield in this cosmic battle.

When Jesus said, "But I tell you, love your enemies and pray for those who persecute you, so that you may be children of your Father in heaven" (Matt. 5:44–45a), he was giving us the cure. He was also telling us something that he himself was deeply familiar with.

In calling Christians to endure persecution faithfully, the apostle Peter pointed them to the example of Christ, who "also suffered for you, leaving you an example" (1 Pet. 2:21). What does it look like to suffer like Jesus? "He did not commit sin, and no deceit was found in his mouth; when he was insulted, he did not insult in return; when he suffered, he did not threaten but entrusted himself to the one who judges justly" (1 Pet. 2:22–23). Jesus doesn't command us to do what he hasn't already done. He went before us and endured persecution without sinning in return, without lying, without insulting, and without trying to take judgment into his own hands. He trusted God and loved his persecutors.

Through the Holy Spirit's power, we can do the same. And when we love our enemies and pray for those who persecute us, we are not only pointing them to the gospel of Christ; we are administering divine healing into our souls.

It's as if loving and praying for our enemies fortifies our hearts against the disease that has infected the people who are persecuting us. The more we love and pray for those who persecute us, the more we are healed and the more we stop the spread of that disease. It's as if we become medicine to our society. This is the good life.

Imagine

Imagine what it would be like to be so lost in being the beloved of God that we find ourselves becoming unoffendable? This is the good life, because our internal joy is not found in external circumstances, but in the eternal God of love. This is the purest form of happiness. The magnificence of our triune God's beauty captures our gaze. No wonder the psalmist said, "Those who look to him are radiant with joy; their faces will never be ashamed" (Ps. 34:5).

Persecution can't steal our joy because our joy never came from our circumstances in the first place. We are looking at God, not our surroundings. He even takes the ups and downs of life and reshapes them into a blessing that makes us more like who we were meant to be. Even when we lose, we win. Why? Because in God's kingdom there is no losing, only lessons that teach and equip us.

> For the LORD God is a sun and shield.
> The LORD grants favor and honor;
> he does not withhold the good
> from those who live with integrity.
> Happy is the person who trusts in you,
> LORD of Armies! (Ps. 84:11–12)

─────────────── Marinate on This ───────────────

Prayer

Lord Jesus,

I do not want to suffer or experience persecution.
But I also know that you said, "You are blessed
when they insult you and persecute you and
falsely say every kind of evil against you because
of me. Be glad and rejoice, because your reward
is great in heaven."

Holy Spirit,

Give me the grace to trust Jesus, even when I do
not understand.

Give me the grace to obey King Jesus when it's
hard and hurtful.

Father,

Clothe me in your presence.

Hold me in your power.

May the fragrance of happiness accompany me.

In Jesus' name, amen

Questions for Reflection

1. Do you view persecution in the name of Jesus as an honor? Do you see persecution producing endurance in your life or the life of others?

2. In Acts 1:8, Jesus commands his followers to be his witnesses in Jerusalem, Judea, Samaria, and to the end of the earth. His followers, however, chose to stay put. What did God allow to happen to them in order that they might scatter? How was God's redemptive plan fulfilled through persecution?

3. Have you ever experienced any kind of backlash because of your faith? How did that make you feel? What was your response? How can you choose to walk with Jesus through these painful experiences?

4. Does it make you nervous to know that life with Jesus will be fraught with trials and persecution? What or Who brings comfort?

5. Praying for our enemies fortifies our hearts against the disease that has infected those who are persecuting us. How can you love and pray for your enemies today?

Things to Remember

1. In Christ, we are a resilient and remarkable people because our God is resilient and remarkable.

2. I believe our post-Christian culture is a fertile environment for the church in America to experience revival.

3. In God's sovereign goodness, he will take persecution and use it to teach us how to rely on him to provide.

4. Life on the margins requires a deeper level of understanding of the beauty of our faith, a higher commitment to be the church in the world, and a stronger cultivation of discipleship.

5. God scattered his Jewish people through persecution so he could gather Gentiles into his family.

6. The holy fire of revival will be one of prayer, ethnic reconciliation, mercy, mission, and holistic discipleship.

CONCLUSION

The Happiness Manifesto

T hank you for taking this sacred journey with me. I know
your time is valuable. I know you are being pulled in a
thousand different directions. I pray that you have found our time
together profitable and beneficial. And I hope that, like old friends,
you will come back and visit with me by rereading *The Good Life*. I
pray that my book would become a friend and companion on your
journey to happiness.

I also want to thank you for joining God the Holy Spirit in
making me a better, happier man. As I typed every word, I had you
in mind. But as I poured myself out in the labor pains of delivering
this baby—I mean book—Jesus was doing something in me. Like
a sculptor, Jesus was shaping, molding, and forging my heart into
his likeness. As I wrote and spent time with him in the Beatitudes,
I discovered that I was becoming more tender, more gentle, more
compassionate, more loving, and more intoxicated with him. I
found myself having a happiness that went beyond the surface of
my circumstances to the depths of my being. As I experienced God
rejoicing over me, his joy became my joy.

"The LORD your God is among you,
a warrior who saves.
He will rejoice over you with gladness.

He will be quiet in his love.
He will delight in you with singing." (Zeph. 3:17)

Our God is a happy God, a singing God who rejoices over his children. His love quiets our fussy souls. It's his love and delight in us that transform us. The good life is a life of being loved by Love himself.

> My lips will glorify you
> because your faithful love is better than life.
> So I will bless you as long as I live;
> at your name, I will lift up my hands.
> You satisfy me as with rich food;
> my mouth will praise you with joyful lips.
> (Ps. 63:3–5)

It is my prayer that your deepest longings will be met by the deep love of Christ Jesus. Your happiness and my happiness are not found in happenings; they are found in the crucified, resurrected King of glory.

> I pray that he may grant you, according to the riches of his glory, to be strengthened with power in your inner being through his Spirit, and that Christ may dwell in your hearts through faith. I pray that you, being rooted and firmly established in love, may be able to comprehend with all the saints what is the length and width, height and depth of God's love, and to know Christ's love that surpasses knowledge, so that you may be filled with all the fullness of God. (Eph. 3:16–19)

Manifesto

When I was in tenth grade, I transferred high schools. This was one of the hardest and best decisions I ever made. My friends from my old high school were not happy with me. They abandoned me. I guess they felt like I abandoned them. I get it. Sometimes life is complicated.

One sad night, I sat in my bedroom with feelings of loneliness and doubt. Could I be successful at this new school? In the midst of this moment, I wrote these words: "I Want To Be The Best Ever." I then took that paper and taped it above my bedroom door. Every morning when I woke up, I saw those words, and every night when I went to bed, I saw them again. Those seven words became my manifesto. It was a public declaration of what I planned to do and become.

In my home, I have "The Dewey Room." (Dewey is my nickname.) This room is filled with pictures and awards of my football career from high school, to college, to the NFL. But my most prized possession is that seven-word manifesto I wrote to myself on October 14, 1986.

In the same spirit, I want to give you a *Happiness Manifesto*. Maybe you can put these words over the door of your bedroom as a source of inspiration and encouragement.

I, _____ ,

declare that all I would ever hope to be is found
in all of who Jesus is. My life is hidden in his
life. His life is my life.

As a gift of grace, Jesus lived a sinless life because
I couldn't.

In his unending mercy, Jesus died the death I should have to atone for my sin. Today, I am free from the power of sin and death.

Because of his great love for me, I am a holy, blameless, righteous, adopted child of God. I am pleasing to the Father because I am in his beloved Son.

The happiness I seek can never be satisfied by created things.

The happiness I was created to experience is not found in happenings.

True happiness is more about God making me good than good things happening to me.

Today, I declare that I choose happiness because I choose Jesus, his kingdom, and his glory.

Today, I declare that I will choose the ways of his kingdom, the truth of his gospel, and live from his life.

Signed _____

Date _____

Thirty-Day Happiness Challenge

One of the spiritual rhythms of grace that has helped in my happiness quest is soaking and immersing myself in Scripture. For the next thirty days, I want you to read Matthew 5:1–12. Read it slowly and prayerfully. Don't rush; take your time. Just because our culture moves fast doesn't mean you have to. Moving at a break-neck pace is surely going to cause us to miss grace. Grace is so unbelievable that we must slow down, sit down, and turn around to see God face-to-face.

Marinate on and soak yourself in Jesus' happiness manifesto in Matthew 5:1–12. Reading Scripture slowly and prayerfully is called *Lectio Divina*. This is a Latin phrase that means "sacred reading." The Father, the Son, and the Spirit want us to have intimacy with them, "into-me-you-see," so we can hear divine whispers of grace. The more we spend time reflecting on Matthew 5:1–12, the more we wallpaper our minds with his thoughts and ways, and by faith his thoughts and his ways become ours. This is the good life. The apostle Paul said, "Do not be conformed to this age, but be trans-formed by the renewing of your mind, so that you may discern what is the good, pleasing, and perfect will of God" (Rom. 12:2).

You want to be happy. I want to be happy. I hope you see that God wants us to be happy too. But the Jesus-kind-of-happiness is vastly different from our culture's thin version of happiness. Jesus' happiness is rooted in our participating and sharing in his life and his kingdom. The happiness that Jesus offers is found in being transformed into a kingdom-of-God-kind-of-person. As we get nearer to the King's heart, we begin to dance to the rhythm of his grace and his character rubs off on us, and we begin to image forth his glory into the world. This is the good life.

> You reveal the path of life to me;
> In your presence is abundant joy;
> at your right hand are eternal pleasures. (Ps. 16:11)

Notes

Chapter 1: Chasing Shadows

1. Carlin Flora, "The Pursuit of Happiness," *Psychology Today*, https://www.psychologytoday.com/us/articles/200901/the-pursuit-happiness (accessed June 12, 2019).

2. Ibid.

3. David Shimmer, "Yale's Most Popular Class Ever: Happiness," *The New York Times*, https://www.nytimes.com/2018/01/26/nyregion/at-yale-class-on-happiness-draws-huge-crowd-laurie-santos.html (accessed June 20, 2019).

4. Ibid.

5. Ibid.

6. Ibid.

7. Jimmy Nguyen, "University Offers Courses in Happiness, Will Count Toward Degree," iHeart.com, https://channel933.iheart.com/content/university-offers-courses-in-happiness-will-count-toward-degree/?Keyid=socialflow&Pname=local_social&Sc=editorial (accessed June 6, 2019).

8. Ibid.

9. C. S. Lewis, *Mere Christianity* (San Francisco: Harper Collins, 1952), 136–37.

10. Scot McKnight, *The Story of God Bible Commentary: The Sermon on the Mount* (Grand Rapids: Zondervan, 2013), 53.

11. Ibid., 38.

12. Ken Boa, *Face to Face: Praying the Scriptures for Intimate Worship* (Grand Rapids, Zondervan, 1997), x.

13. W. W. Wessel, *Blessed*, in D. R. W. Wood, I. H. Marshall, A. R. Millard, J. I. Packer, and D. J. Wiseman, eds., *New Bible Dictionary*, 3rd ed. (Leicester, England; Downers Grove, IL: InterVarsity Press, 1996), 142.

14. R. J. Utley, *The First Christian Primer: Matthew*, vol. 9 (Marshall, TX: Bible Lessons International, 2000), 36.

15. Dallas Willard, *The Divine Conspiracy* (New York: Harper Collins Publishers, 1997), 120–21.

16. Lewis, *Mere Christianity*, 48.

17. McKnight, *The Story of God*, 51.

Chapter 2: Happy Are the Beggars

1. Ken Blanchard and Phil Hodges, *Lead Like Jesus* (Nashville: Thomas Nelson, 2008), 42.

2. R. J. Utley, *The First Christian Primer: Matthew*, vol. 9 (Marshall, TX: Bible Lessons International, 2000), 36.

3. Scot McKnight, *The Story of God Bible Commentary: The Sermon on the Mount* (Grand Rapids: Zondervan, 2013), 39.

4. Ibid.

Chapter 3: Happy Are the Sad

1. R. J. Utley, *The First Christian Primer: Matthew*, vol. 9 (Marshall, TX: Bible Lessons International, 2000), 37.

2. I interviewed Abigail on July 21, 2019, at Transformation Church. View my interview of Abigail here: http://transformationchurch.tc/watch /latest-sermon/.

3. Derwin L. Gray, *Limitless Life: You Are More Than Your Past When God Holds Your Future* (Nashville: Thomas Nelson, 2013), 64.

4. Ibid., 65.

5. Bryan Stevenson, *Just Mercy* (New York: Spiegel & Grau, 2015), 13.

6. Ibid.

7. Ibid., 4.

8. Ibid., 5.

9. Ibid.

10. Ibid.

11. Ibid., 6

12. Ibid., 12.

13. Ibid., 18.

14. Martin Sander, "Bryan Stevenson: 4 Steps to Really Change the World," https://www.christiantoday.com/article/bryan-stevenson-four -steps-to-really-change-the-world/59211.htm (accessed July 24, 2019).

15. Laura Coulter, "Connecting with the Struggle," https://www .evangelicalsforsocialaction.org/compassion-and-justice/connecting-with -the-struggle/ (accessed July 24, 2019).

16. https://eji.org/bryan-stevenson.

17. Ibid.

18. Ibid.

19. Stevenson, *Just Mercy*, 18.

20. To learn more about God's desire to build his multiethnic church, see my book, *The High Definition Leader: Building Multiethnic Churches in a Multiethnic World* (Nashville: Thomas Nelson, 2015).

Chapter 4: Happy Are the Humble

1. J. D. Barry, D. Mangum, D. R. Brown, M. S. Heiser, M. Custis, E. Ritzema, and D. Bomar, eds., *Faithlife Study Bible* (Bellingham, WA: Lexham Press, 2012, 2016), Matthew 16:13.

2. Dr. Martin Luther King Jr., "The Drum Major Instinct," delivered at the Ebenezer Baptist Church, Atlanta, Georgia, February 4, 1968; https://www.cityyear.org/about-us/culture-values/founding-stories/everybody-can-be-great.

Chapter 5: Happy Are the Hungry and Thirsty

1. Jason Silverstein, "There have been more mass shootings than days this year," https://www.cbsnews.com/news/mass-shootings-2019-more-mass-shootings-than-days-so-far-this-year/ (accessed August 7, 2019).

2. Harvard Medical School, "The Homeless Mentally Ill," https://www.health.harvard.edu/newsletter_article/The_homeless_mentally_ill (accessed August 7, 2019).

3. Samaritan's Feet, "Why Shoes," https://www.samaritansfeet.org/why-shoes/ (accessed August 7, 2019).

4. Ibid.

5. Fredrick Buechner, https://www.goodreads.com/quotes/140448-the-place-god-calls-you-to-is-the-place-where (accessed August 8, 2019).

6. Institute for Religious Study Baylor University, "Can a Faith-based Prison Reduce Recidivism?" http://www.baylorisr.org/2012/04/13/%E2%80%9Ccan-an-a-faith-based-prison-reduce-recidivism%E2%80%9D/ (accessed August 8, 2019).

7. Rodney Stark, *The Rise of Christianity* (New York: Harper One, 1996), 161.

8. Ibid., 87.

Chapter 6: Happy Are the Merciful

1. R. J. Utley, *The Gospel According to Luke*, vol. 3A (Marshall, TX: Bible Lessons International, 2004); Luke 10:30.

2. N. T. Wright, *Paul and the Faithfulness of God* (Minneapolis: Fortress Press, 2013), 1445.

3. Ibid; Utley, *The Gospel According to Luke*, Luke 10:35.

Chapter 7: Happy Are the Pure

1. See Transformation Church Values at http://transformationchurch.tc/about/vision-values/.

Chapter 8: Happy Are the Peacemakers

1. Allison Abrams, "How a Toxic Work Environment Affects Your Mental Health, https://www.verywellmind.com/how-a-toxic-work-environment-may-affect-mental-health-4165338 (Accessed September 1, 2019).

2. Ibid.

3. Ibid.

4. Mayo Clinic Staff, "Forgiveness: Letting Go of Grudges and Bitterness," https://www.mayoclinic.org/healthy-lifestyle/adult-health/in-depth/forgiveness/art-20047692 (accessed September 1, 2019).

5. Elle Kaplan, "Why Negative People Are Literally Killing You (and How to Protect Your Positivity)," https://medium.com/the-mission/why-negative-people-are-literally-killing-you-and-how-to-obliterate-pessimism-from-your-life-eb85fadced87 (accessed September 1, 2019).

6. Mayo Clinic Staff, "Forgiveness."

7. Fred Sanders, *Wesley on the Christian Life* (Wheaton: Crossway, 2013), 86–87.

8. Thomas Tarrants, "I Was a Violent Klansman Who Deserved to Die," https://www.christianitytoday.com/ct/2019/september/thomas-tarrants-consumed-hate-redeemed-love-klansman.html (accessed September 4, 2019).

9. Ibid.

10. Ibid.

11. Ibid.

12. John Perkins, *One Blood: A Parting Word to the Church on Race* (Chicago: Moody, 2018), 33.

13. Thomas Kidd and Barry Hankins, *Baptists in America* (New York: Oxford University Press, 2015), 224.

14. Tarrants, "I Was a Violent Klansman."

15. Ibid.

16. Lisa Sharon Harper, *The Good Gospel: How Everything Wrong Can Be Made Right* (New York: Waterbrook, 2015), 140.

17. Tarrants, "I Was a Violent Klansman."

18. Ibid.

19. Ibid.

20. Ibid.

21. Ibid.

22. Michael Emerson cited in Mark DeYmaz, *HUP*, 8. See https://www.markdeymaz.com/glue/2011/08/should-pastors-accept-or-reject-the-hup.html.

23. Scot McKnight, *A Fellowship of Different* (Grand Rapids: Zondervan, 2014), 16.

24. Robert P. Jones, *The End of White Christian America* (New York: Simon & Schuster, 2016), 160.

25. Learn more about the HD Leader Roundtable. We would love to host and connect with your senior leadership team. https://www.derwinlgray.com/hd-roundtable-open.

Chapter 9: Happy Are the Persecuted

1. Associated Press, "Evangelical Christians Wonder Where the Hell Their Power Went," https://nypost.com/2016/06/09/evangelical-christians-wonder-where-the-hell-their-power-went/?utm_source=fark&utm_medium=website&utm_content=link (accessed September 10, 2019).

2. Barna Group, "The Most Post Christian Cities in America: 2017," https://www.barna.com/research/post-christian-cities-america-2017/ (accessed 9.12.19).

3. Lindy Lowry, "Stories of Persecution," https://www.opendoorsusa.org/christian-persecution/stories/myanmar-drops-complaint-against-pastor-who-called-out-abuses-to-trump/ (accessed September 17, 2019).

4. Ibid.

5. To learn about global persecution of the church, see https://www.persecution.com/.

6. Rodney Stark, *The Rise of Christianity* (New York: Harper One, 1996), 3.

7. R. J. Utley, *Luke the Historian: The Book of Acts* (Marshall, TX: Bible Lessons International, 2003), 3B:13.

About the Author

Derwin L. Gray is the founding and lead pastor of Transformation Church (www.TransformationChurch.tc), a multiethnic, multigenerational, mission-shaped community in Indian Land, South Carolina, just south of Charlotte, North Carolina.

Gray met his wife, Vicki, at Brigham Young University (BYU). They have been married since 1992 and have two adult children, Presley and Jeremiah. After graduating from BYU, he played professional football in the National Football League for five years with the Indianapolis Colts (1993–1997) and one year with the Carolina Panthers (1998).

In 2008, Gray graduated from Southern Evangelical Seminary magna cum laude, with a Master of Divinity with a concentration in Apologetics, where he was mentored by renowned theologian and philosopher Dr. Norman Geisler. In 2018, Gray received his Doctor of Ministry in the New Testament in Context at Northern Seminary under Dr. Scot McNight. In 2015, he was awarded an honorary doctorate from Southern Evangelical Seminary.

Gray is the author of *Hero: Unleashing God's Power in a Man's Heart* (2009), *Limitless Life: You Are More Than Your Past When God Holds Your Future* (2013), *Crazy Grace for Crazy Times* Bible Study (2015), and *The High-Definition Leader* (2015).

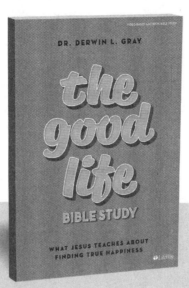

SHARE THE GOOD LIFE

True happiness comes from a heart directed toward the kingdom of God. This is an important message for the body of Christ, so why not share it with your small group? The eight-session Bible study, *The Good Life*, uses teaching videos and personal study to help participants realize the road to happiness is found in the Beatitudes of Jesus.

THE GOOD LIFE LEADER KIT INCLUDES:
- One *Bible Study Book*
- One DVD with a promotional video and eight 9- to 12-minute video teaching sessions with author Derwin Gray
- Code for access to digital video downloads and additional resources through Wordsearch Bible
- Social media assets for the group leader
- Promotional content

USE THIS STUDY TO HELP YOUR GROUP:
- Reflect on the timeless truths of the Beatitudes.
- Find the good life available to those who know Jesus Christ.
- Develop endurance when experiencing persecution.
- Learn to depend fully upon God.

> **"** "I preach and teach from the Christian Standard Bible because of the accuracy, precision, and beauty of the text. I'm excited to finally have one translation that is both faithful to the authorial intent of the biblical writers and written in English that communicates to this generation."

DR. DERWIN L. GRAY

Free resources for you!

Are you looking for more truth to help you on your journey to the good life?

Check out DerwinLGray.com

Download the Happiness Manifesto

This free printable will remind you about the true happiness that is found only in Jesus. Print it out, sign your name, and date it so you can always remember when you committed to walking in the happiness for which you were created. Hang it somewhere you will see it often to continually encourage you.

Listen to episodes of the *Marinate on That* podcast.

Dr. Derwin L. Gray will discuss theology, discipleship, leadership, marriage, and the multiethnic church. Listen and subscribe today.

derwinlgray.com/marinate-on-that-podcast